DOSTOYEVSKY

A BEGINNER'S GUIDE

ROSE MILLER

Series Editors
Rob Abbott & Charlie Bell

Hodder & Stoughton

A MEMBER OF THE HODDER HEADLINE GROUP

Orders: please contact Bookpoint Ltd, 39 Milton Park, Abingdon, Oxon OX14 4TD. Telephone: (44) 01235 400400, Fax: (44) 01235 400500. Lines are open from 9.00–6.00, Monday to Saturday, with a 24-hour message answering service. Email address: orders@bookpoint.co.uk

British Library Cataloguing in Publication Data
A catalogue record for this title is available from The British Library

ISBN 0 340 80033 X

First published 2001
Impression number   10 9 8 7 6 5 4 3 2 1
Year 2005 2004 2003 2002 2001

Cover image supplied by Corbis.
Illustrations by Steve Coots.
Typeset by Transet Limited, Coventry, England.
Printed in Great Britain for Hodder & Stoughton Educational, a division of Hodder Headline Plc, 338 Euston Road, London NW1 3BH by Cox & Wyman, Reading, Berks.

CONTENTS

How to use this book

The *Beginner's Guide* series aims to introduce readers to the major writers of the past 500 years. It is assumed that readers will begin with little or no knowledge and will want to go on to explore the subject in other ways.

BEGIN READING THE AUTHOR

This book is a companion guide to Dostoyevsky's major works, it is not a substitute for reading the books themselves. It would be useful if you read at least one of Dostoyevsky's works in parallel, so that you can put theory into practice. This book is divided into sections. After considering how to approach the author's work and a brief biography, we go on to explore some of the main writings and themes before examining some critical approaches to the author. The survey finishes with suggestions for further reading and possible areas of further study.

HOW TO APPROACH UNFAMILIAR OR DIFFICULT TEXTS

Coming across a new writer may seem daunting, but do not be put off. The trick is to persevere. Much good writing is multi-layered and complex. It is precisely this diversity and complexity that makes literature rewarding and exhilarating.

Literature often needs to be read more than once and in different ways. These ways can include: a leisurely and superficial reading to get the main ideas and narrative; a slower more detailed reading focusing on the nuances of the text, concentrating on what appear to be key passages; and reading in a random way, moving back and forth through the text to examine such things as themes or narrative or characterization. Every reader has an individual approach but undoubtedly the best way to extract the most from a text is to read it several times.

With complex texts it may be necessary to read in short chunks. When it comes to tackling difficult words or concepts it is often enough to guess in context on the first reading, making a more detailed study using a dictionary or book of critical concepts on later readings. If you prefer to look up unusual words as you go along, be careful that you do not disrupt the flow of the text and your concentration.

VOCABULARY

You will see that keywords and unfamiliar words are set in **bold** text. These words are defined and explained in the glossary to be found at the back of the book. In order to help you further we have also included a summary of each section.

You can read this introductory guide in its entirety or dip in wherever suits you. You can read it in any order. It is a tool to help you appreciate a key figure in literature. We hope you enjoy reading it and find it useful.

✻✻✻✻SUMMARY ✻✻✻✻

To maximize the use of this book:

- Read the author's work.

- Read it several times in different ways.

- Be open to innovative or unusual forms of writing.

- Persevere.

Rob Abbott and Charlie Bell

Why read Dostoyevsky today?

HIS ENDURING APPEAL

Dostoyevsky was a writer who achieved cult status in his own lifetime but does his work still entice readers today? Certainly, attendance figures at a recent London film festival devoted to the works of Dostoyevsky indicate something of his enduring reputation. Films such as the three-hour version of *The Brothers Karamazov* (Pyrev, 1968) and the unfinished film of *The Idiot* (Pyrev, 1957) attracted lengthy queues of hopeful viewers and most of them had to be turned away. And yet, how can we account for reactions such as: 'Oh yes, such a great writer, but I haven't read him for years.' Or even, 'He's a fascinating writer, but a bit of a challenge, isn't he?' Such ambivalent responses to Dostoyevsky indicate something of the enduring impact of the writer but also the demands he seems to make upon us. A novel by Dostoyevsky could hardly be described as an easy read. That said, for those who have experienced his work at some stage of their lives, the news of a film season dedicated to his works becomes a positive inducement to go and join a queue! This book aims to explore some of the qualities that are distinctive about his writing, focusing on the particular insight and skill of this complex and arguably somewhat challenging author.

FIRST-HAND EXPERIENCE

Central to the plot of any of his novels is the writer with a fervent social conscience committed to the significance of first-hand experience. The intimate chronicle of deprivation so conspicuous in *Poor Folk* and *Crime and Punishment* was drawn from an environment which Dostoyevsky understood only too well. We know that his active response to the social conditions he deplored led to his arrest and conviction for left-wing activities. A reprieve from the death penalty arrived only at the last minute, but he still spent four years in prison and another six in enforced military service. Dostoyevsky's remaining years were assailed by tortured affairs, the temptation of gambling, prolonged financial constraints and epilepsy, conditions which influenced aspects of all his later novels.

CHARACTER DRAMA

The impact of the drama of his own life can be sensed in the compelling urgency expressed through his characters; their desperate yearning, intense joy, frustration and anguish. These are individuals who are driven, even as he was, by a sense of the fragility and vulnerability of their lives. Dostoyevsky has an ability to draw upon internal conflicts to create beings who express extremes of emotion. Their lives are constrained by circumstances beyond their control. Characters with obsessions are of particular interest to him and we find most veins of neurosis anticipated and explored long before psychoanalysis became an established mode of understanding. From the most depraved to the most altruistic, he portrays characters who, above all, demand something from life, if only a clue to the dilemma of their own existence.

Universal issues

His own dilemma is expressed through his characters in philosophical and ethical debates which remain issues of crucial concern even now. The problems of moral responsibility, the relationship between spiritual belief and ethics, the conflict between personal convictions and political ideology; there seems to be no issue he leaves untouched which does not have relevance to the concerns of our own time.

MASTER OF SUSPENSE

Dostoyevsky is a master of suspense and this must be the key to the success of his longer works. The art of gradual revelation is certainly a strategy he understands thoroughly. Why else do we remain in anticipation for nearly nine chapters of *The Idiot* before our introduction to Nastasya or reach the final verdict on the trial of Mitya only in the last few pages of *The Brothers Karamazov*? Suspense is punctuated, sometimes enhanced and prolonged by the incorporation of the so-called 'scandal' scenes; gatherings or meetings in unusual settings that act as a catalyst to release potent interactions between potentially antithetical or antagonistic characters.

CONTRASTING CHARACTERS

Part of Dostoyevsky's skill in such scenes lies in his ability to contrast and set off one character against another. In *The Idiot*, it is the contrast between Myshkin and Rogozhin which accentuates the sense of crisis in the lives of these two conflicting personalities. And in *Crime and Punishment* it is the relationship between Raskolnikov and Sonya that underlines the inherent link between his transgression and her 'sin'. They contrast, but also complement one another.

INTENSITY

If one had to sum up in one word a vital characteristic of Dostoyevsky's writing, it would have to be intensity. Dostoyevsky is deeply engrossed in his characters, the events he relates and the issues and debates that arise during the course of his narratives. Even when he adopts the position of the detached narrator or chronicler, as in *The Brothers Karamazov* or *The Idiot*, he sustains a sense of involvement in the developing drama of events. The driving force of his engagement creates a sense of inner momentum and accelerated pace which is held in check only by the protracted interactions of the characters. Dostoyevsky seems to want to test their responses in situations that open up critical issues and debates, creating a broader context for the unfolding drama of the narrative. The prolonged speeches and heated arguments of the protagonists can sometimes demand considerable perseverance. Sooner or later, it becomes apparent that every spoken interaction forms an integral part of the dynamic and vivid narrative which is 'orchestrated' for us.

INSIGHT

Albert Camus revered Dostoyevsky as a great prophet of the twentieth century. Sylvia Plath wrote a dissertation on *The Double*. Evidence enough that Dostoyevsky anticipates issues of alienation and identity which have become concerns more closely associated with a twentieth-century predicament. Dostoyevsky retains his hold on our imagination through his profound insight into the human condition transfused with the compassion of a man who suffers even as he writes. Such a compelling writer transcends the historical and cultural dimensions of his era, articulating a life experience which remains as cogent for us as it was to readers in his own lifetime.

✷✷✷✷SUMMARY ✷✷✷✷

- Dostoyevsky is still valued as a significant writer today.
- His works are based on first-hand experience.
- The characters express extreme states.
- Universal issues are a critical focus of exploration.
- Dostoyevsky is a master of suspense.
- Contrasting characters are set beside each other.
- 'Intensity' sums up the overall approach of Dostoyevsky.
- He anticipates issues that concern us today.

How to approach Dostoyevsky's work

2

START WITH *POOR FOLK*

Dostoyevsky was fascinated by people. His novels are populated with characters who resemble the people he knew, characters derived from newspaper articles and even characters inspired by other novels.

Reading the works of Victor Hugo, Charles Dickens and Gogol, all novelists whose works he loved, would be one way to begin to understand Dostoyevsky. The most direct way to approach Dostoyevsky would be to start with his very first published work, an **epistolary novel** called *Poor Folk*.

> **KEYWORD**
>
> Epistolary novel: a novel written in the style of letters exchanged between characters.

ADVANTAGES OF LETTERS

There is something very immediate and accessible about letters. Even in our era of telecommunications letters continue to be written and received, if not by post, then by e-mail. Correspondence between friends, even in published form, retains a sense of intimacy, an ease of communication which reveals more, sometimes, than face-to-face encounters. Perhaps this is the reason why the epistolary novel became so successful as a genre. During the eighteenth century, the epistolary novels of Samuel Richardson were so popular that they were translated into four languages. Dostoyevsky was certainly familiar with them. For a young writer, then, it is hardly surprising that his first original work took this form. The success of *Poor Folk* owes much to the way in which the epistolary novel suited the ideas and feelings that Dostoyevsky was striving to convey. For the reader looking for an introduction to Dostoyevsky, *Poor Folk* presents some characteristic features of his style in an accessible form.

A PARTICULAR POINT OF VIEW

A letter to a friend can present a very personal perception of the world. Dostoyevsky was very concerned in all his novels to help the reader see the particular point of view of his main characters as a factor which determines their actions. In *Poor Folk*, this idea is virtually spelled out for us. In a series of letters the reader shares the hesitancy, doubts, anxieties and moments of joy expressed in a developing intimacy between the two correspondents. Makar and Varvara are relatively uneducated, providing an excuse for the fresh, informal style of their correspondence. Their letters may appear to be unsubtle, but this is a device that highlights the contrast between the two. It also draws attention to the divergent approaches adopted by each character in an effort to resolve their difficulties.

SELF-CONSCIOUSNESS

The particular point of view of the character includes, of course, a particular view of oneself. What becomes obvious at an early stage is that Makar is afflicted with the most agonizing self-consciousness. Bakhtin points out that in the typical Dostoyevsky character, the reader sees 'not who he is, but *how* he is conscious of himself' (Bakhtin, M., 1984, *Problems of Dostoyevsky's Poetics*, Manchester University Press, p.49). He perceives this difference to be crucial to an understanding of all Dostoyevsky's work. It sets him apart from other nineteenth-century writers, including Gogol, a writer who is often cited as the inspiration for *Poor Folk*.

DIVIDED PERSONALITY

How does Makar perceive himself, then? Apparently with doubt. In this humble clerk dignity and integrity coexist with incipient fallibility and weakness. Humiliated by a sense of his unworthiness, he struggles to improve himself and yet cannot resist succumbing at least once to the consolation of the bottle. The feelings expressed in his letters range from exuberance and elation to the most cowering abjection and misery. This polarism of the dynamics of personality was to become more evident in Dostoyevsky's subsequent works, affecting not only characterization but the overall sense of pace and emotional climate.

Makar has an interview with his Excellency.

GRADUAL REVELATION

From the very first page, the reader is immersed in an established personal correspondence between Makar and Varvara. There is no introduction and no intervening explanations are made by a narrator. This leaves a great deal for the reader to deduce. The content of the letters makes it possible to piece together the background and details of the relationship. However, this process does take some time, because information is either omitted or taken for granted. In subsequent works, Dostoyevsky develops the approach of gradual revelation to activate the reader's curiosity, to build up a sense of anticipation or to heighten a feeling of suspense.

STORIES WITHIN STORIES

The letters trace the ensuing stages of a relationship but function also as a narrative frame in which Dostoyevsky situates related stories surrounding the lives of the two main characters. We find benign recollections of Varvara's rural childhood, the tale of Makar's youthful follies and amours and a heart-rending account of a destitute family in Makar's lodging. The sense of lives which have been frustrated, efforts impeded, the oppression of poverty on mind and spirit becomes all the more evident set beside accounts of happier times or simple descriptions of incidents recalling the capacity for enjoyment of these two unfortunate correspondents.

SOCIAL CONCERNS

Dostoyevsky was appalled by the conditions of the working classes and used *Poor Folk* as a means of drawing attention to the crippling effects of poverty. On a personal level this is conveyed by the desperate attempts of Varvara and Makar to manage on too little or their fruitless efforts to cover up the full extent of their difficulties. When Varvara admonishes Makar for sending her a pot of geraniums we begin to appreciate the sacrifice that such a small gesture entails. Eventually, the problems of such an existence become insurmountable. The decision that Varvara takes is both inevitable and tragic, an ultimate protest by the author against the economic and social constraints dictating the lives of these poor people.

Lack of Closure

Dostoyevsky disliked writing endings for his works and in *Poor Folk* it is already evident how much he sought to mirror the inconclusive nature of real life. Major changes in Varvara's circumstances bring about an abrupt termination of her correspondence with Makar. The reader is left with a few hints as to the most likely future developments in her life but has to speculate about Makar's prospects. A sense of rupture, of a relationship relentlessly crushed by fate resonates through Makar's last entreaty:

You must write to me again … otherwise, this will be my last letter; and, I mean, it's impossible that this letter should be my last. I mean, how can it be, so suddenly, my last?

(*Poor Folk*, p.129)

***** SUMMARY ** *** **

- *Poor Folk* is Dostoyevsky's first published novel.

- As an epistolary novel, it is easy to read and a useful introduction to his work.

- *Poor Folk* demonstrates features of Dostoyevsky's style, such as:
  - Presenting the story through the point of view of the characters
  - Characters with divided person-alities
  - Gradual revelation
  - The use of a narrative frame to include other stories
  - Social concerns
  - Lack of closure

3
Biography: a life on the edge

INFLUENCE OF LIFE HISTORY

There are some writers whose works we can appreciate without knowing anything of their biographical details. Others seem to be endowed with the potential to arouse intense curiosity about every aspect of their lives. Dostoyevsky is one such writer. In his case, the dramatic events of his life were of such momentous impact that his writing and indeed his ability to write were both affected. Having survived a near-death experience and years of imprisonment, his subsequent writing was irrevocably shaped by these experiences. There is also the significant issue of his physical condition to take into account. For most of his life, Dostoyevsky suffered from epilepsy, an affliction which, in his case, followed a pattern of recurrent seizures succeeded by long periods of recovery. His tortuous grasp of his own physical and mental resources imbued his writing with an underlying sense of urgency, an awareness of the fragility of life. Writing was, for Dostoyevsky, a tool for survival. It was through his writing that his life experiences could be absorbed, examined and assimilated. A look at the chronology of his life will underline the extent to which it informed and inspired his work.

EARLY LIFE

Dostoyevsky's parents belonged to those educated fringes of the middle classes who, during the nineteenth century, struggled to lead a barely comfortable life. His father was a doctor at the Moscow Shelter for the Poor, where Dostoyevsky was born in 1821, and his mother was the daughter of a merchant. The family, eventually consisting of eight children, lived in a two-bedroom apartment attached to the refuge. By 1831 his father had achieved a greater measure of financial security and was able to invest in a small country property called Darovoe. Here the family spent their summers in what seemed like idyllic surroundings to the young Dostoyevsky. The death of his mother in 1837 brought this happier period of his life to an end. His father resigned from his post and took the four youngest children to live with him at Darovoe. Dostoyevsky and his brother were sent to the St Petersburg Military Engineering Academy where he endured rather than enjoyed a disciplined educational regime.

A SUDDEN DEATH

The most traumatic event of this period was the sudden death of his father in 1839, a tragedy heightened by what he considered to be the unresolved circumstances surrounding his death. Dostoyevsky and his brother Andrei suspected that he may have been murdered by his own serfs, although this remained unproven. There is some conjecture that the real cause of death was alcoholic poisoning or even a heart attack precipitated by the letter announcing Dostoyevsky's first year exam failure at the Academy. The unresolved problems of his relationship with his father emerged many years later in *The Brothers Karamazov*, a novel in which patricide became a major theme. It was after his father's death that Dostoyevsky began to suffer from the epilepsy with which he was afflicted for the rest of his life.

FIRST SUCCESS

In 1844 Dostoyevsky left his post with the engineering corps, staking his future on his ability to survive as a writer. It must have been rewarding to achieve an instant success with *Poor Folk*, his very first and perhaps most painstaking effort to write a short novel. *Poor Folk* was hailed as the work of a genius in the eulogizing reviews which accompanied publication of the work. Unfortunately, this lucky break was succeeded by less than enthusiastic reviews of his subsequent stories 'The Double' and 'The Landlady'.

PRISON AND ITS AFTERMATH

Often dismissed today as a derivative work, *Poor Folk* nevertheless expresses with great poignancy the constraints in the lives of a social group which Dostoyevsky had observed at close quarters. It seems evident that the fictionalized portrayal of these lives of dejection was not a sufficient outlet for the expression of his concern. During the late 1840s he became more active politically, attending secret meetings of the Petrashevsky circle, a socialist group that advocated freedom of the press and the liberation of the serfs. These were certainly dangerous principles to uphold at a time of repressive official response to recent political upheavals throughout Europe. In 1849 Dostoyevsky and 34 members of this group were arrested and incarcerated in St Peter and St Paul Prison, a fortress reserved for the most dangerous state criminals. After some months of investigations, most of the group were condemned to death.

The list of criminal offences of which Dostoyevsky himself was accused ranged from criminal conspiracy and planning to setting up an underground publishing house to making abusive remarks about the Orthodox Church and government. It is generally accepted now that the execution by firing squad was staged in order to teach the 'anarchists' a lesson. If so, it must have been an effective performance, for Dostoyevsky was certainly convinced of the reality of the event. An acquaintance he met some years later recalled the profound impact the experience still had on him as he relived the event for her:

And then some unknown voice pronounced: 'You are sentenced to execution by shooting.' We were surrounded by a crowd of several thousand faces, red from the cold, and thousands of inquisitive eyes … All were excited … All were excited about life. And we had to face death … I did not believe it. I did not understand it until I saw a priest carrying a cross … I then clearly understood that death was inevitable. I wanted everything to be over as soon as possible … Suddenly I became indifferent to everything … It all seemed so insignificant in comparison with transferring to another state, to some darkness … Without any joy whatsoever, without emotion, we received the announcement that the execution had been cancelled.

(Sekirin, P., 1997, *The Dostoyevsky Archive*,
McFarland & Company, p.196)

Although the death sentence was revoked at the last minute by the Czar, Dostoyevsky still had four years of a prison sentence to endure. Between 1850 and 1854 he was detained in Omsk maximum security prison. Chains were worn day and night, the diet of cabbage soup was almost exclusive and no books were allowed except for the *New Testament*. In a letter to his friend, Apollon Maikov, he describes the frustration of the experience:

> I cannot express to you how much I suffered from not being able to write in prison. The whole time I was there, my work simmered inside of me.

> (*ibid*, p.111)

Memoirs from the House of the Dead, a fictionalized account of these experiences, appeared in the newspaper *Russian World* from 1860.

Dostoyevsky went through a mock execution.

RETURN FROM EXILE

Released from prison, Dostoyevsky was ordered to go into military service for the next six years, remaining in Siberia to serve as a private in the Infantry. At least he was able to read and write again. Strangely enough, the long period of incarceration had brought about a complete reversal of his political stance. To one friend of this period he expressed the view that the Russian people were not yet ready for a Western-style constitutional government. Dostoyevsky became a monarchist, writing patriotic poems which were passed on by his friends to appropriate officials in government circles. He also met Maria Isaeva, who became his wife in 1857. At this time he suffered epileptic attacks about once a month. Supported by friends, he petitioned Czar Alexander, a measure which obtained his discharge from the army on medical grounds.

In 1859 Dostoyevsky was permitted to settle in St Petersburg, where his time was divided between editing literary journals and writing; an intensive lifestyle in which he often worked all night long in order to meet deadlines. During this period he published *Notes from Underground* (1862), a work which is distinctively self-critical, attacking the idealism and romanticism of his earlier years. His public readings from the work attracted much controversial attention, but were received with enthusiasm by young audiences.

ROMANCE AND ROULETTE

It was during the winter of 1862 that he became intimate with fellow writer Apollinaria Suslova, the woman who inspired some of the most intriguing female protagonists of his subsequent novels. She was a young **narodnik**, enthusiastic about the emancipation of women, and a confirmed **nihilist**. In 1863 he followed 'Polina' to Europe, catching up with her in Paris to resume a tempestuous relationship

KEYWORDS

Narodnik: a person affiliated to a populist group that promoted education for the peasants and a back-to-basics approach to Russian culture.

Nihilist: a person who rejects all traditional religious and moral principles. Nihilists in Dostoyevsky's period also upheld extreme political views.

Dostoyevsky enjoyed gambling.

only rivalled by his newly discovered passion for roulette. Circumstances were against him: Polina took up with a younger man and Dostoyevsky's wife became seriously afflicted with tuberculosis. Returning to her bedside, he remained in attendance until she died in 1864, a fateful year which also marked the death of his brother Mikhail. Dostoyevsky was left with his brother's family to support, together with a legacy of debt. At this time he was still tenuously involved with Polina but beginning to long for a more sustainable relationship, a situation which was to remain unresolved despite several attempts to form new alliances. This is the period of *Crime and Punishment*, the story of a young man driven through poverty and misplaced ideology to commit murder and his subsequent salvation through the agency of a woman. In what was to become a characteristic gesture of an inherent perfectionist, he burned the first version. Dostoyevsky was later to incinerate manuscripts of *The Idiot*, *The Eternal Husband* and *The Demons* in one go.

HIGH STAKES

With such extreme standards, the need to meet publication deadlines was a source of particular anguish. Dostoyevsky himself was distressed by the inconsistencies that emerged in his novels, the lack of clarity in certain parts, the rough edges in others; all the result of hasty submissions to his editors, chapter by chapter. These deadlines were a necessity, for he was always in dire need of the payments for his writing. But in a sense they were also self-imposed. The stake all or lose all mentality of the gambler was in his blood, an attribute of his lifestyle. A bout of gambling in 1865 contributed to the financial crisis which soon drew him into signing a rash contract with his publisher. The terms were to deliver a complete new novel within the space of a month or forfeit the copyright on all his existing works. He managed to complete *The Gambler* within a hair's breadth of the deadline. An unexpected bonus emerging from this winning streak was the acquisition of a new wife. Anna Snitkina was the young stenographer he employed while writing *The Gambler* and whom he subsequently married. She seemed to have the patience and forbearance to cope with his vacillating condition. Gambling lapses were always succeeded by intense periods of remorse and depression.

AN ÉMIGRÉ EXISTENCE

In the early months of 1867 Dostoyevsky began to suffer from more acute bouts of epilepsy and obtained official permission to seek treatment in Western European clinics. In fact, the financial crisis faced by him at this time necessitated a long period abroad to escape the importunate demands of creditors. *The Possessed* and *The Idiot* were written during this period of émigré existence as the couple moved between Geneva, Berlin, Dresden, Prague, Milan and Florence. Such an itinerant lifestyle may have had a beneficial effect on his health but it increased his exposure to the lure of the casinos. Gambling remained a potential addiction to which he still yielded occasionally, but inevitably with catastrophic results. The writing of his final version of *The Idiot* took place during a year in which, on one occasion, he staked and lost his coat, his wedding ring and all his money.

For a writer living on the brink of catastrophe, a permanent threshold of physical and material collapse, the need to remain in contact with his cultural heritage became an imperative. Encounters with fellow émigrés, letters from friends and relatives in his homeland and the avid perusal of Russian newspapers provided a stabilizing influence, as well as support and sustenance for his writing. All the novels and articles of this period of residence abroad convey a distinctive sense of his Russian identity.

RECOGNITION AND ACHIEVEMENT

In 1873 Dostoyevsky agreed to become editor of *The Citizen*, returning to St Petersburg to carry out this engagement, but recurrent health problems forced him to relinquish the post after a few years. He did, however, resume publishing *A Writer's Diary*, a popular journal which began its life as part of *The Citizen*. By now Dostoyevsky was beginning to attract the attention of the 'establishment'. In 1877 he was elected a member of the Academy of Sciences and he became an esteemed and frequent guest at the Winter Palace in St Petersburg. By 1880 his popularity as a national cultural figure was undisputed and police surveillance of his activities was finally terminated. The most dramatic and memorable event of this period was undoubtedly his speech to mark the opening of the Pushkin Memorial in 1880. Surviving eye-witness accounts of this event are unanimous in acknowledging the sense of empathy and the stirring feelings that Dostoyevsky inspired in his audience. The hysterical ovation inspired by his address was a token not only of public esteem for a great Russian poet, but a confirmation of Dostoyevsky's charismatic presence and popularity as a great literary figure.

A FINAL TRIBUTE

Dostoyevsky's final novel, *The Brothers Karamazov*, was the only work he was able to write in relative financial solvency. The reprieve did not last long. In 1881, just a few months before the assassination of Czar Alexander II, Dostoyevsky died, leaving the completed text of Part I and some notes for the envisaged Part II. The funeral was a tremendous event: newspapers reported the largest public gathering in Russia for the whole of the nineteenth century with 50,000 people paying their last respects. Mourning went on for a whole month with ceremonies and meetings commemorating his death, one of them distinguished by funeral music improvised by the composer Modeste Mussorgsky (1839 –81). Such a prolonged public expression of bereavement was in itself an admirable tribute to the achievements of a writer whose career had been fraught with almost overwhelming obstacles.

✳ ✳ ✳ ✳ SUMMARY ✳ ✳ ✳ ✳

- His mother died when he was 16 and his father died two years later.

- Epilepsy became an affliction that affected him for the rest of his life.

- Involvement with the Petrashevsky circle led to his arrest and imprisonment.

- He was sentenced to death, but reprieved at the last minute.

- He spent four years in prison and six years in enforced military service.

- He married Anna Snitkina, the stenographer employed to write up *The Gambler*.

- His final years in St Petersburg marked the height of his success as an editor and renowned author.

- Dostoyevsky died in 1881.

Major works

4

CRIME AND PUNISHMENT
Unlikely material
An impoverished ex-student, idealistic, ambitious and frustrated by the material constraints of his life, forms the resolution to murder an old pawnbroker and avail himself of some ready cash to resolve his difficulties. This is hardly an optimistic or encouraging start for a novel that goes on to describe the development and realization of this hideous scheme and its aftermath. Nevertheless, in 1866, *Crime and Punishment* was acclaimed as the literary sensation of the year, its serial publication provoking storms of controversy.

A psychological drama
It must be said that *Crime and Punishment* recounts the story of a crime without becoming a punishment to read. Dostoyevsky achieves this through a masterly exposition of the complex psychological state of a man driven to commit a desperate act. Keith Carabine has pointed out the significance of early drafts indicating that Dostoyevsky was originally planning to write a confessional style novel (Carabine, K., 2000, *Crime and Punishment,* Introduction and Notes, Wordsworth Editions). This can be perceived as evidence of Dostoyevsky's concern for the reader to experience virtual identification with the psychological state of a character in crisis. Even though Dostoyevsky settled eventually on the use of a narrator, the sense of proximity and total involvement is almost uncanny. With the most compelling penetration, Dostoyevsky projects the brooding anxieties of Raskolnikov, his hesitations and doubts, the alienation and distortion of reality induced by inertia and depression.

Divided consciousness

The ideological concerns reflect some of the topical debates surrounding the activities of nihilists and radical thinkers of Dostoyevsky's time. In the narrative, these arguments develop into obsessions, activated by several events that all happen at the same time and play upon his sense of predestination. First, he overhears a student literally articulating his own thoughts. The end justifies the means, he declares, citing an old pawnbroker as a parasite on society who should be eliminated. Her life is of no benefit to anyone; her money could be used to help those who really need it. Soon after this Raskolnikov happens to find out that the sister of the old woman will be out of the apartment at a certain time. Dostoyevsky draws out the simultaneous sense of compulsion and dissociation which takes over from this point. Raskolnikov has convinced himself of the logical justification for the murder. However, his sense of morality acknowledges the monstrous absurdity of such an act. His divided state is such that the reader is left in doubt until the last minute as to whether the deed will take place.

Psychic disintegration

Dostoyevsky explores Raskolnikov's oscillating emotional reactions to the crime with compelling persuasion. An instinctive cunning prevents him from betraying himself in escaping the scene of the crimes and sheer panic leads him to hide the stolen goods under a huge stone. Yet, when summoned to the police station to pay his debts issued on a promissory note, he feels an overwhelming urge to confess to the superintendent. Visiting Razumikhin, a close friend, he becomes unaccountably abusive and hostile, behaviour which his friend can only attribute to a delirious fever. A conflicting succession of violent emotional reactions ranging from paranoia to intense self-revulsion take possession of him. As he roams the streets of St Petersburg his environment absorbs the harsh and sombre colours of his projected feelings. His divided consciousness makes it impossible either to live with the consequences of his action or to admit his guilt.

Complicity

The reader, as the only witness to the murder, is drawn into a complicit alliance with Raskolnikov, responding to the double entendre of language, the potential suspicion latent in the words of friends and associates. Dostoyevsky plays upon this uncertainty to considerable effect in the interviews with Porfiry, a police superintendent of the new school, who undertakes to explain his theories of criminal behaviour to Raskolnikov. It becomes impossible to ascertain whether Porfiry is convinced of Raskolnikov's guilt and is leading him on or is merely suspicious of him and trying to find out more. Raskolnikov treats these encounters like tactical assaults, exposing significant details, making contentious statements. In a chance meeting with Zamyotov, a government official, he even specifies how the murder would have been accomplished had he done it. The inside-out perspective of Raskolnikov's world comes to dominate every aspect of the narrative, absorbing the complicit reader into the operations of his tortured mind.

Significance of Sonya

Sonya Marmeladov becomes an increasingly significant figure in Raskolnikov's life as he makes frantic attempts to comprehend the nature of his deed. At first she seems to be adopted as his logical symbolic counterpart whom he accuses and punishes as his own alter ego. Aware of the degrading profession she was forced to adopt, he expostulates:

> You've done the same thing, after all, haven't you? You've also stepped across ... found it in yourself to step across. You've committed moral suicide, you've wrecked a life ... *your own.*

> (Part IV, Chapter 4)

The anguish he experiences for both of them is centred on an ideological dilemma which appears to be insoluble in his terms. Of what use is self-sacrifice if it achieves nothing? The murder he committed was a sacrifice of a human life and also a form of moral self-sacrifice. Yet it accomplished nothing and was essentially a useless act. Sonya takes on the role of a confessor, the first person to whom Raskolnikov relates the account of the murders and the **proto-Nietzschean** 'will to power' that led him to take such an extreme measure. She is the one who articulates the feelings that he has refused to acknowledge in himself. Profoundly disturbed by his confession, she asks him to go to the crossroads, to kiss the ground that he has desecrated, to proclaim his sin. Raskolnikov refuses to acknowledge his guilt in a world which he perceives to be run according

KEYWORD

Nietzsche: a German philosopher (1844–1900) who argued that ideas and actions are given a reality through an assertion of 'will'. His works were not published before 1872. Raskolnikov's ideas are proto-Nietzschean, that is, in anticipation of the ideas of Nietzsche.

to principles of power and appropriation. Just for a moment, however, he is almost able to weep, a sign that her concern has been recognized in some deeper level of his being.

Theatre of the absurd

Dostoyevsky contrasts and contextualizes Raskolnikov's obsessive condition through the interpolation of striking incidents ranging from the strange to the bizarre. These events serve to introduce comic or eccentric characters or to provoke extraordinary interactions between

Katrina and her children dance for scraps.

existing characters. Take, for example, the ridiculous presentation of Luzhin as Dunya's proposed fiancé in Part II, or Razumikhin's eager attempt to set up a love nest for his friend Zosimov in Part III. These are both incidents that interrupt the prolonged tension of the narrative and create a sense of relativity and incongruity. As the narrative pace accelerates, these insertions take on more of the dynamics of tragic absurdity.

In Part V, Sonya's stepmother takes to the streets in demented hysteria, forcing her terrified children to sing and dance for their supper. When Raskolnikov attempts his major act of penance at the crossroads in Part VI, spectators mock him, assuming that he must be drunk. In the most disturbing of these accounts, Dostoyevsky traces the nocturnal wanderings of Svidrigailov after he has failed to blackmail and seduce Dunya. So distraught is his condition that it becomes impossible to distinguish between reality and dream, a condition that distorts the reader's own perception of the narrative events. The suicide scene adds a final touch of grotesque irony:

> He put the revolver to his right temple.
>
> 'Vat-z-you doing, here is impossible, here is not ze place!' Achilles said, rousing himself and dilating his pupils wider and wider.
>
> (Part VI, Chapter 6)

Rashkolnikov prostrates himself in the market.

Confession or defeat?

Dostoyevsky, to the very end, avoids obvious solutions to the problems that beset his protagonists. Here is no case of contrition and remorse or the converse position of obdurate denial. Raskolnikov finally gives up because all other doors seem to be closed. Circumstances almost demand it. Unaware of Svidrigailov's recent activities, he decides to confess in order to terminate the power of that man over his sister. But even at this vital moment the outcome remains uncertain. Hearing that Svidrigailov has committed suicide, Raskolnikov nearly changes his mind and actually leaves the police station. Only the expression on Sonya's face as she becomes aware of his omission stirs him to return and make an unequivocal deposition.

Humiliation

It is shame rather than remorse that haunts Raskolnikov during the first year of his eight-year prison sentence. Shame provoked by his failure to execute a plan which seemed a logical and necessary consequence of his convictions. His irresolute behaviour and his weakness in capitulation torment his wounded pride. Unreconciled to the past, the future seems of equal futility. He cannot even resolve the ethical dilemmas activated by the failure of his endeavour. Dostoyevsky certainly manages to avoid the pathos of the 'reformed penitent' so beloved by romantic novelists. Redemption is a tenuous thread on the horizon which Raskolnikov only begins to grasp as the narrative draws to an end.

A lament

Crime and Punishment is infused with a sense of urgent social concerns and contemporary political issues. There is the character of Marmeladov, inspired by the anti-alcohol journalism of the period. The grinding poverty of Marmeladov's family and that of Raskolnikov himself reflects the state of financial crisis in St Petersburg at this time. It is not surprising then, that the novel was interpreted by critics of his day as an indictment of the nihilist beliefs of students and extremists reacting to these conditions. In fact, this was not Dostoyevsky's purpose at all. He made it clear that the novel was conceived as a 'lament' rather than a reproach or a condemnation. The criticism implicit in the narrative reflects upon his own past as much as the unrest of his younger contemporaries. In the end, *Crime and Punishment* transcends the nature of its intention, remaining to this day one of the most widely read of all Dostoyevsky's works.

THE IDIOT

Conception of the work

Is it possible to write a convincing story about a 'positively good person'? In a letter to his niece (January, 1868) Dostoyevsky attempts to clarify the nature of the problem: 'There is only one positively good man in the world, and that is Christ' (*World's Classics*, Introduction, Oxford University Press), adding that such an exemplary model is almost impossible to emulate in literature. This was the challenge motivating the conception of *The Idiot*, a novel which underwent eight drafts as Dostoyevsky struggled to personify the presence of goodness in an incompatible world. Even after he had completed and sent off Part I, Dostoyevsky remained dissatisfied with his attempts to address this problem. Yet, of all his novels, *The Idiot* was the one he cherished most. It is the story of an uncorrupted man of compassion and humility who fails to realize his idealistic convictions. It retains the flavour of an allegory retold in the form of a **realistic novel**.

> **KEYWORD**
>
> Realistic novel: a fictional attempt to convey the effect of realism through the interaction of characters of a specific social class in everyday situations.

Pure theatre

> He seems to have been chosen by the destiny of Russian letters to become Russia's greatest playwright, but he took the wrong turning and wrote novels.
>
> (Nabokov, V., 1983, *Lectures on Russian Literature*, Pan, p.104)

Far from taking a wrong turning, Dostoyevsky's sense of drama, so apparent in *The Idiot*, is what makes his works so alive. The novel begins with a scene which in terms of character interaction can best be described as pure theatre. Set in a third-class railway carriage, the scene functions as an anonymous venue that isolates the characters from their usual surroundings. Myshkin and Rogozhin are presented through descriptions of their appearance, as if seen through the eyes of a fellow passenger. The reader, as this anonymous passenger, absorbs the image of Myshkin with his bundle, his insufficient cloak and expectant air of naive enthusiasm. Dostoyevsky brings out the contrast in appearance and demeanour between Myshkin and Rogozhin as an indication of their divergent characters. Yet there is a recognition of mutual compatibility as the conversation develops, a rapport that arises naturally from the context and interaction of character, as in live theatre. The dialogue between them also informs the reader about the woman who will become significant in both their lives. Lebedyev's interruptions add a material contribution; his obsequious behaviour towards Rogozhin and dubious treatment of Myshkin indicate the relative social status each is ascribed in the eyes of the world:

> Prince Myshkin? Lev Nikolayevich? I don't know it, sir. I can't say as I've even heard of it, sir.
>
> > (Part I, Chapter 1)

By the end of this scene, the reader knows enough about the characters and situation to be able to contextualize subsequent events.

Dark and light heroines

Myshkin and Rogozhin are not the only characters set in such striking contrast to each other. Dostoyevsky's heroines are also typically polarized. Nastasya is the dark-haired fiery beauty, the victimized 'femme fatale', uncertain whether to encourage or to punish her admirers. Aglaya (light) is the innocent, capricious young girl, whose beauty Myshkin is in awe of from the first encounter:

> You are extraordinarily beautiful, Aglaya Ivanovna. You're so pretty, one is afraid to look at you.
>
> > (Part I, Chapter 7)

Dostoyevsky avoids the obvious stereotyping of character by underlining the identity of Nastasya as a victim (of Totsky, her seducer). Aglaya, though innocent, is certainly no angel, as demonstrated in her recitation of the Pushkin poem 'The Poor Knight', an obvious parody of the Prince and his attempts to rescue Nastasya (Part II, Chapter 7). Myshkin's relationship with Nastasya becomes a threatening undercurrent that undermines his rather tenuous relationship with Aglaya. Inevitably, the first and last meeting between these two rivals becomes a highly fraught confrontation brought to a head by Nastasya's ultimatum:

> If he doesn't come up to me, now, take me, and give you up, then you can have him. I'll let you have him. I don't want him.
>
> (Part IV, Chapter 8).

Appalled by her distraught condition, Myshkin hesitates just long enough to convince Aglaya that he prefers Nastasya. He never really recovers from the sense of having made an irrecoverable mistake. The interview with Radomsky after the event reveals the tragic irony of his situation. Unable to explain the difference between his fearful compassion for Nastasya and his love for Aglaya, he is obliged to live with his dilemma, accepting its consequences in the eyes of the world.

The Holy Fool

'We are fools for Christ's sake' exhorts St Paul (I Corinthians, 4:10). When Rogozhin exclaims on first parting from Myshkin: 'You're an out-and-out holy fool, and God loves the likes of you!' (Part I, Chapter 1), he is teasing Myshkin but also invoking this tradition. Indeed, Myshkin could be perceived as an unconscious **Holy Fool**, denounced as an idiot by Ganya (Part I, Chapter 7) and indulged as a wayward child by the Yepanchin's guests (Part IV, Chapter 7). Most of the novel underlines

KEYWORD

Holy Fool: This was the tradition of kenoticism that emerged in the Russian Orthodox Church during the fourteenth century, where the 'holy fool' practised a kind of radical asceticism, irrationality, could feign madness and was inspired by a gift of prophecy.

the discrepancy between the Christian ethics the Prince strives to practise and the reality of the ways of the world. His words and activities seem to be constantly misunderstood, creating difficulties where they might not otherwise exist, often compounded by his incorrigible goodwill and obliviousness. At one stage, Aglaya confronts Myshkin with the disconcerting news that his attentions are so excessive that everyone assumes he will marry her. Given full rein to express his vision of harmony, the results are catastrophic, as in the evening party at the Yepanchins, where, in his excitement, he breaks a valuable vase and has an epileptic fit (Part IV, Chapter 7). In spite of all this, Dostoyevsky succeeds in creating a 'positively good' character who inspires both sympathy and respect. Aglaya herself confirms that:

> I have never in my life met a man like him for noble simplicity, and boundless trustfulness.

(Part IV, Chapter 8)

The difficulties experienced by Myshkin also express Dostoyevsky's recognition of the limitations of idealism in a world which significantly fails to countenance such ideals.

Autobiographical elements

The Idiot, more than any other novel, draws on aspects of Dostoyevsky's own life. The descriptions of Myshkin's epileptic fits are communicated with the vivid conviction of personal experience. Myshkin's account of the scaffold scene witnessed at Lyons (Part I, Chapter 5) parallels features of Dostoyevsky's own experience as a condemned man. Even the characters are often drawn from real life. Nastasya bears a striking resemblance to Apollinaria Suslova, the compelling woman Dostoyevsky was involved with during the 1860s. There are less obtrusive but equally interesting correspondences. Dostoyevsky spent many years away from St Petersburg, either in prison or seeking treatment abroad. Myshkin was a virtual prisoner of his illness, undergoing treatment abroad for many years. Both Myshkin and Dostoyevsky were expert calligraphers. The novel also features descriptions of Holbein's 'The Dead Christ', a painting that made a profound impact on Dostoyevsky when he saw it in Basel. In a vivid depiction of the realistic rendering of Christ's body, Ippolyt interprets His death as an act of sacrifice which seems to have been in vain. Could this be an analogy intended as a premonition?

Function of scandal scenes

The dramatically charged, disruptive encounter between two or more divergent, antipathetic individuals is a characteristic feature of Dostoyevsky's mature style. The intensity of the occasion creates a change of direction in the flow of events, when heated arguments, accusations and declarations reach a climax, contributing towards unforeseen developments of the narrative. These **scandal scenes**, or 'conclaves', focus on incongruous meetings and bizarre interactions as an integral dynamic feature which activates change:

> **KEYWORD**
>
> Scandal scene: a dramatic, disruptive encounter between two or more characters.

> People appear for a moment outside the usual conditions of their lives, on the carnival square or in the nether world, and there opens up another – more genuine – sense of themselves and of their relationships to one another.'
>
> (Bakhtin, M., 1984, *Problems of Dostoyevsky's Poetics*, Manchester University Press, p.145)

Two significant examples

An example of such a scene occurs when Nastasya visits Ganya's family (Part I, Chapter 9). Her sudden appearance precipitates a row between brother and sister absurdly contrasted by the embarrassing overtures of Ganya's alcoholic father. The arrival of Rogozhin with his rowdy cohorts adds a further bizarre contribution to the general hysteria. The confrontation forces Ganya to clarify his intentions, demonstrates Nastasya's volatile temperament, but more significantly, introduces Myshkin to Nastasya for the first time.

The ultimate scandal scene takes place at Nastasya's name-day party (Part I, Chapters 15 and 16), an event which seems to anticipate solutions to a number of difficulties. What Dostoyevsky does is to bring together everyone who hopes to gain something from Nastasya that evening. Totsky, her guardian and seducer, hopes to secure his freedom by marrying her to Ganya. Yepanchin hopes, without much faith, to make her his mistress. Rogozhin, the merchant, hopes to return with 100,000 roubles to buy her. Myshkin is the only person to make a proposal that is totally selfless, generated by his compassionate love and admiration. The discovery of the Prince's inheritance transforms this extraordinary declaration into something out of a fairy tale. Nastasya, unfortunately, cannot perceive it as anything but that. She astounds her guests by turning down the Prince and choosing Rogozhin when he appears with the loot. In her parting gesture of defiance, she flings Rogozhin's bundle of roubles onto the fire, challenging Ganya to take them as a gift if he can retrieve them barehanded. Its a statement that denounces her suitors and their mercenary intentions in one blow.

A compendium of stories

In scandal scenes, characters are virtually ignited by the shock of confrontation. But Dostoyevsky never stops searching for situations which can contribute towards the reader's understanding of a character. Much is revealed, also, by stories which characters tell each other in **interpolated narratives**. The poignant real-life story of Marie which Myshkin recounts to the Yepanchin women reveals his sublime compassion for anyone who suffers (Part I, Chapter 6). The accounts of Burdovsky's claim to Myshkin's inheritance are absurd interventions illustrating the methods of opportunism and the gullibility of innocence (Part II, Chapter 8). By the time Ivolgin treats him to a rambling monologue about his experiences with Napoleon, Myshkin is aware enough to feel acute embarrassment, knowing something, by then, of the ways of the world (Part IV, Chapter 4).

KEYWORD

Interpolated narratives: stories told by characters which interrupt, complement or digress from the main plot of the novel.

Use of the narrator

At certain points, Dostoyevsky interrupts the narrative pace to describe events through the medium of an anonymous narrator. This is a deliberate device, which has several vital functions in the novel. First, it creates a separation between each part or between significant events, rather like a staged soliloquy between acts of a play. In the opening of Part III, for example, the narrator reflects on those who distrust non-conformity, with Madame Yepanchin particularly in mind. This sets a general tone of disharmony in which the Prince's attempts to reconcile his antagonistic friends meets with disapproval. The use of a narrator also creates a sense of distance from the events taking place. It is an agreeable change after the highly charged scandal scenes and whirlwind pace of events in some parts of the novel. Distance is achieved through objectivity and detachment. The narrator merely reports, stating what is known or unknown, sometimes including rumour and heresy. In Part IV, Chapter 9 the narrator acts as a discrete society columnist, informing the reader of the embellished and distorted interpretations of the Prince's activities. He consolidates conflicting rumours, reports and letters, to piece together the events surrounding Nastasya's last flight. For the reader, this is ideal preparation for the events which follow.

The uncanny

There are times when Dostoyevsky draws on all his resources to build up an atmosphere of suspense, creating a disturbing sense of anxiety, a sense of the **uncanny** which is projected into the anticipated narrative events.

> **KEYWORD**
>
> Uncanny: the ordinary world made strange and sinister.

When Myshkin reappears after an absence of six months (Part II, Chapter 2), Dostoyevsky envelops his activities with an undercurrent of foreboding. There is the 'strange hot stare of eyes in the crowd' noticed by Myshkin on his arrival at the station, the oppressive atmosphere of Rogozhin's gloomy house and the morbid despair of his monologue. Details are significant too. The knife that

Rogozhin toys with becomes an obsessive object of attention for Myshkin. In spite of professing friendship and an exchange of crosses, the lingering sense of some impending calamity possesses him. Myshkin becomes increasingly agitated without being able to understand why as he paces the streets wondering what to do next. The

Myshkin is attacked by Roghozin.

attack by Rogozhin followed by Myshkin's violent epileptic seizure brings the chapter to a climactic resolution.

A memorable scene

Such a blood-curdling event is merely a rehearsal for the final chapter of Part IV. Here Dostoyevsky draws his inspiration from a newspaper report of a notorious murder case, infusing the narrative with elements of **Gothic fiction** and his own

KEYWORD

Gothic fiction: a term used to describe fiction infused with a brooding atmosphere of blood and terror reminiscent of the gothic novels of Anne Radcliffe, William Beckford and Matthew Lewis.

sense of the uncanny to effect a powerful conclusion. All the warning signs are there: the glimpse of a face peering out surreptitiously from one of the windows of Rogozhin's house, the strange, furtive behaviour and air of preoccupation exhibited by Rogozhin when Myshkin encounters him. Why does Rogozhin insist that they enter the house so quietly? And why is the room so dark? The descriptive sequence of Myshkin's subsequent observations is spine chilling in its gradual revelation of the scene he encounters. A strange vigil follows, which compounds the sense of horror as both men gradually suffer a complete derangement of their faculties.

A novel about failure?

The reader is left to resolve the issues that Dostoyevsky opens up in *The Idiot*. Is the work a failure in its attempt to realize the character of a positively good person? Is Myshkin as the 'hero' a failure as a character, because he was too unrealistic about the power of goodness? Do his friends and associates fail to appreciate sufficiently the essential goodness in Myshkin? The attraction of the novel lies precisely in its power to evoke these ethical dilemmas without providing a prescriptive solution.

THE BROTHERS KARAMAZOV

Parricide

The story of the murder of an old man and the conviction of his eldest son as the murderer forms the basis of one of Dostoyevsky's most highly acclaimed novels, the product of his final years of relative prosperity and acclaim. First published in serial form in the *Russian Herald* between 1879 and 1880, *The Brothers Karamazov* came out as a single edition in 1881, the year of his death. Parricide was an issue which concerned Dostoyevsky at intervals throughout his life, stimulated by a variety of factors and influences. That his father died in circumstances which, to him, were not clearly explained, seemed to have left him with a lifelong sense of responsibility for his death. During his years in prison, he became acquainted with a man who had been falsely convicted and served ten years for the murder of his father before he was reprieved. Literary influences made their contribution as well. He knew *The Robbers*, a play by Schiller, and *Mauprat*, a novel by George Sand, both of which feature the subject of parricide. Yet the assumption that *The Brothers Karamazov* represents Dostoyevsky's final attempt to grapple with this theme is contradicted by the author's own preface to the first edition.

One hero or three conflicting characters?

In his preface, Dostoyevsky makes it clear that he had originally planned a second volume featuring Alyosha as the hero. The intention of the first volume was to provide a background to his life, a 'moment from Alyosha's early youth'. Alyosha seems to have been conceived as a more well-rounded version of Myshkin in *The Idiot*. In fact, the sequence of dramatic narrative events foregrounds Dmitri and Ivan as much if not more than Alyosha. *The Brothers Karamazov* is really a novel with three main protagonists, each distinctly contrasting in personality and approach to life. The differences between the characters of the brothers have tempted many critics to interpret them symbolically in terms of three distinct types. Mitya, the confirmed rake represents the sensualist, Ivan the theorist is the intellectual and Alyosha, the virtuous man, represents spiritual life. Such a reductive generalization hardly does justice to the complexity of these characters and certainly takes no account of their interaction. The strength of the novel lies, not in the characterization as such, but in the way Dostoyevsky uses these contrasting characters to explore some of the central issues activated by the events of the narrative.

A crime story

The account of the circumstances leading up to the murder of Fyodor Pavlovich, together with the subsequent events, forms the narrative structure of a great drama packed with suspense. It remains as compelling today as it was on first publication. Dostoyevsky deliberately builds up a misleading sense of anticipation through his description of the behaviour of Dmitri, the oldest son. With the motive and expressed intention to murder reinforced by the expectations of his associates, the deed becomes a virtual *fait accompli*. His father, after all, was trying to appropriate Dmitri's woman (Grushenka) as well as money that Dmitri considered to be his own. They had argued repeatedly and even come to blows. If the story had been that predictable, however, it would hardly have been so intriguing. Dostoyevsky introduces elements which raise doubts, initially in the mind of the reader, then in the context of the narrative. Why is Dmitri so astounded when he is accused of murdering his father? Why is Smerdyakov so repulsively insinuating? The conflict of opinions about Dmitri's guilt reaches a climax during the trial, an extraordinary revelation not only of concealed circumstances surrounding the deed but of the methods of justice of the time. The conviction of a suspect seems to be as much to do with the oratory of the prosecutor and defendant as the relative guilt of the accused. Dostoyevsky uses his sense of dramatic occasion to create stirring courtroom scenes of accusation and refutation, hysteria and delirium, all witnessed by an avid crowd of enthralled spectators.

Guilt and responsibility

The long protraction of a courtroom trial parallels the gradual revelation of evidence for the reader. It provides ample opportunity for Dostoyevsky to use the interaction of his characters to explore some of the key issues raised by the murder. If Ivan knew that the murder was a possibility when he left town, does that make him responsible in any way for the murder? Was his deliberate absence, in effect, a form of collusion in the event? If Dmitri did not murder his father, was his careless rage and flagrant expression of intent an incentive or provocation for the person who did accomplish the deed? Was Alyosha also responsible in some way through his lack of active intervention?

The double

Sometimes Dostoyevsky has too much to communicate about a particular individual to conform to prescribed conventions of character and identity. It is almost as if something overflows from one

Ivan has a conversation with the devil.

personality to engender another. Ivan's delirious phantom conversation with the devil is the most striking example of such an excess. In this case, the devil appears as a *doppelgänger*, or a double, representing aspects of Ivan's own divided personality. Ivan is completely convinced of the reality of the confrontation, observing the minute details of the behaviour and appearance of his visitor. Yet he also explains to the bemused Alyosha:

> And he – is me, Alyosha, me myself. All that's low, all that's mean and contemptible in me!

> (Part IV, Bk 11, Chapter 10)

The double functions as a mirror, forcing him to confront aspects of identity and issues of belief which he would otherwise avoid.

A literary compendium

Ivan's conversation with the devil is an example of a particular incident conveyed through a specific approach to writing. It demonstrates Dostoyevsky's concern to present the diverse aspects of a situation by changing his style. *The Brothers Karamazov* actually contains an extraordinary variety of forms of writing which help to communicate this sense of difference. During the period when he was writing this novel there was a vogue for the **feuilleton** in literary publications. His own contribution to the genre was *A Writer's Diary*, a series of magazine-style articles and stories published in the format of a feuilleton which he kept up over a period of nine years. *The Brothers Karamazov* was written during an interruption to this long-term project. Perhaps it is hardly surprising, then, to discover such a range of genre and form included in the text. As well as a crime story and a family chronicle, there is a formal disputation, a parable (in 'An Onion'), confessions, dream visions, satires and reportage, to mention just a few examples. Such diversity adds another multiple dimension to the complex construction of the narrative.

> **KEYWORD**
>
> Feuilleton: a sequence of articles and anecdotes with an integrating commentary published in almanac form. Feuilletons became popular during the 1840s in Europe.

The Grand Inquisitor

The interpolation of the extraordinary interview between Christ and the Grand Inquisitor is illuminating as an indication of Ivan's critical iconoclasm but self-sufficient as an allegorical treatise in its own right (Part II, Book V, Chapter 5). On one level, it seems to be an indictment of the Christian church. However, as the argument is quite elaborately developed and has since been subjected to considerable speculative analysis, it is worth presenting a brief outline of the incident.

Christ comes back to earth unexpectedly, appearing to the common people in the streets of Seville during the Inquisition. The Grand Inquisitor notices that a man is performing miracles illegally and takes prompt action to have him put away. In a midnight visit to his cell, the Inquisitor informs Christ that he is aware of his true identity and specifies the reasons for his detention. He reminds Christ of the three temptations presented to Him by the devil. First, He was asked to demonstrate His miraculous powers by changing bread into stone. Christ refused. Would He leap from the pinnacle of the temple? He refused. Why not assert his power to be able to rule over all the people of the earth? This also Christ refused. By refusing the three temptations, Christ designated His own right to make moral choices. According to the Inquisitor, the Church has had to correct Christ's error of refusal. Ordinary people need mystery, miracle and authority, he contends. They need someone to bow down to, someone to take over their conscience and some way of establishing their common identity. The Grand Inquisitor confesses that the Church has recognized for a long time that there is no God. The legend of Christ is deliberately perpetuated, a myth designed as a control mechanism. The appearance of a real Christ would disrupt the whole edifice of illusion. Therefore it is necessary to eliminate Him. Fortunately, the Inquisitor does not feel obliged to have Christ burnt at the stake but simply commands Him to walk out into the night. After such a grilling, he believes it is unlikely that Christ will be tempted to make any return visits.

This extraordinary reconstruction of the temptation of Christ can be perceived as blasphemy of the highest order. Many critics have interpreted the story in a broader context, however, as a representation of **totalitarianism**. The Grand Inquisitor expresses a totalitarian ideology which strives to repress the terrible freedom of choice which would otherwise become the responsibility of the individual.

KEYWORD

Totalitarianism: relating to a centralized dictatorial form of government which demands complete subservience to the state.

The end is the beginning

Dostoyevsky died before he could write the second volume of *The Brothers Karamazov*. One could argue that the work is self-sufficient in any case. Certainly the epilogue does provide indications of further narrative developments that counteract any sense of final closure. This may be an indication of the direction which Dostoyevsky was intending to pursue or simply the characteristic gesture of an author who hated finishing his work. The final irony is that posterity will never know whether the work is unfinished or whether Dostoyevsky simply changed his mind. Whatever the case, the imperative issues explored in *The Brothers Karamazov*, universal issues of fallibility, human destiny and meaning, remain significant concerns relevant for our time as much as for his.

✵ ✵ ✵ ✵ SUMMARY ✵ ✵ ✵ ✵

- *Crime and Punishment* is the psychological account of a crime.

- Its impact relies on the complicity of the reader.

- *Crime and Punishment* should be perceived as a lament for those who ignore the values of humanism.

- *The Idiot* is inspired by Dostoyevsky's concern to write about a 'positively good person'.

- In *The Idiot* dramatic highly charged scenes activate new directions in the narrative.

- *The Brothers Karamazov* explores Dostoyevsky's concern with the subject of parricide.

- These divergent strands intersect in his formulation of a crime story, featuring three main characters.

- Their interactions during the development of the narrative provide a framework for Dostoyevsky to explore ethical and philosophical concerns.

- *The Brothers Karamazov* is technically incomplete, but it is not absolutely certain that he really intended to finish it.

5 Major themes

THE GREAT UNREST

Temporary residents

Dostoyevsky's experiences in prison drew his attention to a curious behavioural pattern which he observed amongst his fellow inmates. In *Memoirs from the House of the Dead*, the novel he wrote based on these experiences, the main protagonist notices that the prisoners behave as though they are only temporary residents, even the ones who have 20-year sentences to serve.

Restless characters

This sense of the temporary is a more extreme example of a tendency that can be discerned in all his novels. As a mode of being, it enters into the dynamics of context, characterization and narrative development. Dostoyevsky's characters seem to be passing through, moving on, or stopping for the time being in a place which may or may not be of their own choosing. Their restlessness may simply be a response to constrained circumstances, as in the obvious case of the prisoners. Yet it also seems to indicate a more profound level of disturbance. Is it possible to get to the root of this condition by examining the environment and circumstances of his characters?

Distracted

Locating descriptions of the environment of the characters is a more difficult task than one might expect. Nabokov notes:

> If you examine closely any of his works … you will note that the natural background and all things relevant to the perception of the senses hardly exist. What landscape there is, is a landscape of ideas, a moral landscape.
>
> (Nabokov, V., 1983, *Lectures on Russian Literature*, Pan, p.104)

Nabokov perceives this absence of physical data as evidence of Dostoyevsky's limitations as a novelist. The relative disregard for background does convey something of the preoccupation of the author with his characters and their problems. Dostoyevsky writes through the sensations and ideas of his characters, an approach which was perceived by literary critics such as Bakhtin to be fundamental to his work. In these terms, an absence of background reveals the minimal extent to which the characters themselves are aware of their environment. For they are all people with something else on their mind.

Passing through

Dostoyevsky's characters seem to be always on the move. They are in a hurry to be somewhere else, anywhere else, so long as they can keep moving. Settings which they pass through seem to reinforce a sense of mobility and transience. The railway carriage, city streets, bars, busy tenement blocks, extended social gatherings in rooms which are too small, are characteristic venues for people in transit. Like the typical city dwellers of today, Dostoyevsky's characters are immersed in their problems and preoccupations, noticing only what they have time for or cannot avoid. The few descriptions of external setting which he grants us punctuate the text like views through windows in a passing train. They are fleeting glimpses rather than absorbing spectacles. Raskolnikov, in a rare moment, pauses on a bridge over the river Neva to look at the dome of the cathedral. His restless condition makes it impossible for him to take in the immediate impression of the scene. Instead, he becomes immersed in the feeling he used to have about it:

> He always felt an inexplicable coldness drifting towards him from this magnificent panorama; for him, this lavish tableau was full of a tongueless, hollow spirit.
>
> (*Crime and Punishment*, Part II, Chapter 1)

Poet of the metropolis

Dostoyevsky is 'the first and greatest poet of the modern capitalist metropolis', affirms Lukács, confirming a contemporary desire to articulate the tragic predicament of the individual who becomes a victim of urban society (Lukács, G., 1962, ed. Wellek, R., *Dostoyevsky, A Collection of Critical Essays*, Prentice-Hall, p.153). Raskolnikov, above all, lives in contingency mode. His room is temporary, he has abandoned his studies for the time being and he is out of work. The sense of impermanence and dissatisfaction breeds the alienation pervading his consciousness, enhanced by the conditions of his impoverished state. Restlessness takes the form of aimless wandering through the streets while he becomes increasingly preoccupied with manic obsessions and delusions. The resulting murder is an inevitable consequence of such a chain of cause and effect. *Crime and Punishment* is not just a psychological study of the effect of a crime, as Dostoyevsky once claimed, but a study in the effects of alienation. A striking example of this occurs at an early stage of the narrative when Raskolnikov encounters a young inebriated prostitute on the Boulevard. Disgusted by the situation of this young girl who is about to be picked up by an obvious roué, his overwhelming sense of alienation becomes so acute that he soon abandons his attempts to rescue her.

> Why did I poke my nose in, trying to help? Is it for me to do that? Do I have any right to? Oh, they can swallow each other alive for all I care!
>
> (*Crime and Punishment*, Part I, Chapter 4)

Fugitives

The transient, alienated attitude is not simply a reaction to the conditions of urban life. Dostoyevsky's characters in all sorts of environments suffer from a sense of alienation and frustration. Aglaya, reacting against her sheltered life in the Yepanchin household, strives to articulate her inchoate longing for a meaningful existence. Summoning Myshkin, she announces:

I want to run away from home, and I've chosen you to help me ... I want
to be of use. I've been wanting to get away for a long time. For twenty
years I've been bottled up at home, and they keep trying to marry me ...
I want to go to Rome ... I want to study in Paris.

(*The Idiot*, Part III, Chapter 8)

Ganya's discontent takes the form of intense egocentricity, as he
struggles against his limited nature. He is alienated from his own self:

A profound and continual consciousness of his own lack of talent, and
at the same time the overwhelming desire to prove to himself that he was
a man of great independence, had rankled in his heart almost from his
boyhood up.

(*The Idiot*, Part IV, Chapter 1)

Dostoyevsky's characters are tormented by their longing for some
other mode of being yet suffer from an inability to achieve their desire.
Awareness of their situation merely heightens the degree of their
reaction to it. This is the real motivation for the tortuous scandal
scenes and the demonstrative reactions of Nastasya, Katerina, Ganya
and Ivan. Their journeys are flights, their encounters are fugitive and
eruptive. The reactions of these characters express blind panic fuelled
by anguish:

Their despair is an actual banging at closed doors, an embittered, futile
struggle for the meaning of life which is lost or in danger of being lost.

(Lukács, G., 1962, ed. Wellek, R.,
Dostoyevsky, A Collection of Critical Essays, Prentice-Hall, p.156)

No way out

The extraordinary modernity of Dostoyevsky lies partly in his refusal
to formulate a positive solution for his restless characters. In *The Idiot*,
Myshkin suffers a drastic reversal and Aglaya makes a disastrous
marriage. In *The Brothers Karamazov*, Dmitri is sentenced with only a
marginal chance of escape. Dostoyevsky can point towards strategies

for survival, but he never provides the sense of final resolution which traditional plots require.

A modern dilemma

The great restlessness of Dostoyevsky's characters is a condition we can recognize and identify with. Through their discontent, their fugitive condition, their alienation and anguish we hear a voice that anticipates the consciousness of our own era. Albert Camus believed that Dostoyevsky's works were of the greatest relevance to the problems of twentieth-century man. To see these problems presented in the context of Dostoyevsky's world is to be reminded of their significance and of the extended horizon which offers a continual hope of reconciliation.

THE SEARCH FOR CONDITIONS OF PERFECTION

Heights and depths

Prince Myshkin is often pointed out as an example of Dostoyevsky's pursuit of an ideal, an exponent of the perfectly good man he tried to realize in *The Idiot* and afterwards in *The Brothers Karamazov*. Was this much quoted ambition an indication of Dostoyevsky's quest for an ultimate state of perfection? Certainly he did seem to be concerned to portray various caring, self-sacrificing individuals. Myshkin, Sonya, Alyosha and Father Zosima are some of his most significant characters in this respect. If perfection was such an abiding concern, how then does one account for the volume of space he devotes to some of his more than reprehensible characters? Raskolnikov and Svidrigailov plumb the depths of moral fallibility in *Crime and Punishment* and Smerdyakov transmits the worst aspects of criminal opportunism in *The Brothers Karamazov*. Bear in mind, also, that Dostoyevsky had formulated plans to write a series of novels on the 'Life of a Great Sinner'.

Dark and light

In fact Dostoyevsky was intent on exploring the limits of the most negative as well as the most positive aspects of human nature. The concept of perfect goodness is very important in establishing the ultimate parameters of the scale. But the convincing representation of evil is equally important. It was part of his working method to examine all manifestations of any condition. All his other characters found a place somewhere on a scale between the two extremes. There are two questions to resolve here. First of all, why did he adopt this approach? Second, how did his desire to portray a perfectly good man relate to his approach to characterization as a whole?

Diverse influences

Specific influences on his approach are quite hard to identify, simply because Dostoyevsky was such an eclectic and voracious reader. Besides a range of literary texts, he studied philosophy, theology, medicine, psychology and political theory at various times of his life. The range of his researches was considerably enhanced by his duties as an editor. Catteau observes with considerable insight the way in which Dostoyevsky drew his inspiration from a very broad range of ideas and sources:

> The important thing is that he swept them all in together, clasped in each others arms like wrestlers in mortal combat, and stored them all ready for use.
>
> (Catteau, J., 1989, trans. Littlewood, A., *Dostoyevsky and the Process of Literary Creation*, Cambridge University Press, p.76)

The only conceptual ideas which seem to rationalize this breadth of vision would be those presented in the writings of Hegel, though it is evident that this philosopher represented only one of many with whom Dostoyevsky was familiar. Hegel postulated that truth involves contradictions. Truth as an ultimate condition depends on developing a sense of wholeness. This can only be achieved through examining all aspects, including contradictions; in what Hegel described as a **dialectic** process.

KEYWORD

Dialectic: presenting opposite points of view in an argument in order to reach a conclusion.

Thinking through characters

In such terms the diverse characters who populate his novels constitute all the elements of a whole picture, the true picture of reality. Their interactions and conflicting concerns present contrasting aspects of a situation, different problems and perspectives. The development of his narrative through the characters also activates arguments about crucial philosophical, religious, ethical and social issues. Bakhtin believes that:

> It is given to all of Dostoyevsky's characters to 'think and seek higher things'; in each of them there is a 'great and unresolved thought'; all of them must, before all else, 'get a thought straight.' ... If one were to think away the idea in which they live, their image would be totally destroyed.
>
> (Bakhtin, M., 1984, *Problems of Dostoyevsky's Poetics*,
> Manchester University Press, p.87)

The critic Strakhov, who was also a close friend of Dostoyevsky, observed that:

> The most general and abstract thoughts acted on him with great power ... He seemed to feel thoughts with uncommon vividness. Then he would set the thought out in different ways, sometimes giving it a picturesque, arresting image.
>
> (Catteau, J., 1989, *Dostoyevsky and the Process of Literary Creation*,
> Cambridge University Press, p.15)

Dostoyevsky sets his thoughts out mainly through his characters. But he himself is preoccupied in each of his novels with at least one 'great and unresolved thought'. Thoughts about perfection and the limits of perfection seem to be the most difficult to resolve. This may account for the fact that each of the novels surveyed in Chapter 4 is concerned in some way with perfection. Dostoyevsky's need to examine every aspect of the problem emerges in some uncommon approaches to the subject. How does he set this out in practice?

Raskolnikov – the imperfect villain

It is quite apparent that Raskolnikov was never intended to function as a perfect villain. For a start, he was far too conscious of the absurdity of his projected plan. Throughout his preparations for the murder, he is struck by the unfeasible nature of his resolution. In fact:

> The more final they had grown, the more monstrous and absurd they at once became to his eyes.
>
> (*Crime and Punishment*, Part I, Chapter 6)

Then he made a mess of the job, ending up by killing two victims instead of one and forgetting to take most of the loot. This hardly puts him in the running for the man who commits the perfect crime either. Most of the novel is an examination of the consequences of the obsessive idea which possesses Raskolnikov. Having rationalized the perfect justification for the appropriation of wealth, he is bound to act upon it. Even after murdering the two women, Raskolnikov manages to remain convinced of the perfect rationality of his idea. That murder happens to be one of the by-products, does not seem to invalidate his arguments, as far as he is concerned. He is not the perfect villain then, but perhaps he would qualify as the perfect anti-hero. Raskolnikov, in that sense is the hero who has got onto the wrong track, possessed by a misguided idea. To him it seems a perfect solution to the problems of the world.

Smerdyakov – the unscrupulous villain

When it comes to perfectly unscrupulous villains, Smerdyakov is arguably the most completely reprehensible candidate. Everyone has come across a variation on this particular character; the odious individual who has every excuse for his behaviour but who nevertheless fails to evoke an ounce of sympathy. Dostoyevsky avoids the obvious at all times and his characterization of Smerdyakov is a masterpiece of innuendo and insinuation. First, he manages to obtain power over Ivan simply by behaving as though there is some dark secret between them, an assumed complicity giving rise to the sense of conspiracy. Every interaction becomes an exercise in double entendre which is deliberately cultivated by Smerdyakov and ineffectually resisted by Ivan. His parting advice to Ivan:

> 'In your place, if it were me, I'd leave the whole thing right now ... rather than sit next to such business, sir.'
>
> (*The Brothers Karamazov*, Bk V, Part II, Chapter 6)

becomes part of a deadly web of guilt and intrigue designed to protect his own interests. Adding guile to insinuation, he is able to turn Ivan's own arguments into a justification for his crime:

> If there's no infinite God, then there's no virtue either, and no need of it at all ... You yourself kept saying then that everything was permitted, so why are you so troubled now, you yourself, sir?
>
> (*ibid*, Bk II, Part IV, Chapter 8)

Even when Ivan manages to corner him, extracting a confession, he still manages to gain the upper hand by taking ultimate steps to stop his confession getting any further.

Sources of perfect heroes

Models for his less desirable characters, the reprobates, the cynics and sinners were easy enough to find. But how could he represent the opposite end of the scale? Christ was his ideal model for the most perfect example of a good man (see, p.25). Were there other sources which could have inspired him?

There was one 'real-life' chronicle which must have played a part in the development of his perfect character. In 1856 a curious publication called *A Tale of the Monk Parfyony's Wanderings and Travels in Russia, Moldavia, Turkey and the Holy Land* attracted the attention of Dostoyevsky and his contemporaries. Sometimes described as a poetic folk tale, it presents the story of an utterly good, sincere man whose religious fervour and simplicity won the hearts of his readers. Dostoyevsky owned a copy which he took abroad with him during the period in which he was working on *The Idiot*.

A more direct source of inspiration could have been his own nephew. Before going abroad, Dostoyevsky was staying in the same house as Alexander Petrovich Karepin, an unusual young man whose behaviour attracted a certain degree of harmless ridicule. He was passionate about finding an ideal woman and could read *Don Quixote* in the original.

An imperfect perfection

Dostoyevsky, in his turn, became inspired by the implausible character of Don Quixote:

> Of all the beautiful figures in literature, Don Quixote is the most finished. But Don Quixote is beautiful only because he is ridiculous at the same time.
>
> (Catteau, J., 1989, *Dostoyevsky and the Process of Literary Creation*, Cambridge University Press, p.44)

This seems an absurd choice for a perfect character, but it demonstrates how Dostoyevsky appreciated from the start the difficult nature of his task. At the time, he rationalized such a preference as a means of evoking the compassion and sympathy of the reader. Don Quixote became part of the fabric of *The Idiot*, featuring in Aglaya's recitation of Pushkin's verse narrative. The scene is significant in that it underlines an intentional analogy between the chivalrous would-be knight and the misguided interventions of Myshkin (Part II, Chapter 7).

Right from the start, the perfect man is conceived as an individual who deviates to the point of absurdity from established conventions of behaviour. There are other compromises which Dostoyevsky feels obliged to make. Myshkin is not just naive, he is apparently unmoved by physical passions. Straus argues that in Myshkin 'the attempted erasure of sexual desire' is a deliberate move to eliminate physical love in order to substitute spiritual love as an active force binding men and women together (Straus, N., 1994, *Dostoyevsky and the Woman Question*, St Martin's Press, New York, p.56).

If so, the attempt is unsuccessful, for Myshkin loses both Aglaya and Nastasya and in the end, his reason. Indeed, according to Peace, *The Idiot* represents:

> A typical Dostoyevskyan paradox – as a novel it is an artistic success; while as a vehicle for the great idea; the positively good man, it is a failure.

> (Peace, R., 1971, *Dostoyevsky*, Cambridge University Press, p.70)

Alyosha

Is Dostoyevsky more successful with Alyosha in *The Brothers Karamazov*? Like Myshkin, Alyosha imparts a feeling of well-being, something akin to grace, a quality which moves Grushenka to fall to her knees before him. Perhaps Alyosha is more convincing as a representation of the 'perfect' man because Dostoyevsky allows him just a trace of identifiable human failings. Take, for example, Alyosha's reaction to the unpleasant circumstances surrounding the death of Zosima. His almost surly behaviour prompts his friend Rakitin to observe with glee:

> Oho, so that's how we are now! We're snappish, just like other mortals! and we used to be an angel! Well, Alyoshka, you surprise me.

> (Part III, Bk 7, Chapter 2)

But this is a rare slip for a young man renowned for his implacable good nature and solicitude. Strangely enough, despite the impressive length of *The Brothers Karamazov*, Alyosha remains an elusive, even an undeveloped character. He seems to function as a bystander, confidante or a participating observer rather than a protagonist in a narrative that essentially revolves around the implications of a murder. Sources available confirm that Alyosha was destined to play a more active role in a subsequent volume. This would account for the abiding sense of unrealized potential which seems to cling to him.

Perfection of another order

Perfection is the 'great unresolved thought' which Dostoyevsky investigates through his characters. It inhabits Raskolnikov as a misguided ideal and Smerdyakov as the limits of calculated villainy. Through Myshkin and Alyosha, Dostoyevsky examines the problem of perfection in relation to an imperfect world. The 'great unresolved thought' situates the context in which his characters present conflicting aspects of the author's dilemma. Resolution is never achieved and yet, in the process, Dostoyevsky seems to achieve a certain perfection of quite a different order. Perfection does exist in his works in their virtual achievement of the comprehensive. His characters who strive to realize perfection in various ways represent absolutes in a study of an incredibly vast range of interactive characters.

VICTIMS AND VICTORS: THE PROBLEM OF WOMEN

Demonstrative women in Dostoyevsky

The women in Dostoeysky's novels seldom take the leading parts, yet they seem to be determined to make their impact on the development of the narrative. Clamouring for attention in a male-orientated society, they implore and beseech, they rant and rave, revile and condemn. Above all, they seem to be capable of mocking the infirmities of the men who control them. Are these women merely foils for Dostoyevsky's charismatic male protagonists or do they have something to tell us about their own identity and function?

Issues influencing women as characters

There are a number of cultural and personal factors to be taken into consideration. In the 1860s 'the woman question' was already becoming a controversial, even a fashionable issue with certain Russian intellectuals. It was a period when Dostoyevsky had an intense affair with Apollinaria Suslova, a woman of charismatic presence and progressive views. Her influence combined with his long sojourns abroad gave him a more cosmopolitan perspective on the developing awareness of a younger generation of women. At the same time,

Dostoyevsky was deeply concerned about the power of men over women's lives, a control which frequently led to abuse and prostitution. He never forgot the incident during his childhood when a young girl of his acquaintance was raped and then murdered. These factors had an influence on the background and circumstances of some of the female protagonists he wrote about. To some extent, these influences also account for the deeply ambivalent personalities of the women who appear in his novels. Women in Dostoyevsky's novels reflect both his anxiety about womens' potential power and indignation about their continued victimization.

Woman as victim

Crime and Punishment contains some of the most compelling examples of female victimization and degradation. In his wanderings through the streets of St Petersburg, Raskolnikov encounters an inebriated girl who has obviously become a prostitute. The appalling inevitability of her plight is reinforced both by her own hardened indifference and Raskolnikov's half-hearted attempts to rescue her (Part I, Chapter 4). This minor scene brings up the theme of victimized woman which becomes fully developed in the presentation of Sonya. In many respects, she represents the typical 'fallen woman', an innocent girl reduced to prostitution through the desperate poverty of her family. Even before she appears, Dostoyevsky introduces her as a victim of oppressed conditions and male domination. Marmeladov's drunken narration (Part I, Chapter 2) is a recriminating account which reveals his own recurrent appropriation of her hard-earned wages. Sonya's noticeable arrival at the scene of Marmeladov's death reinforces the pathos of her situation. She emerges from the crowd of spectators:

> Tarted up in the manner of the streets, in accordance with tastes and conventions that have developed a peculiar world of their own, with a gaudy and shameful purpose that is all too obvious.
>
> (Part II, Chapter 7)

Subsequent encounters reinforce her vulnerability and humiliation. Encountering Raskolnikov's mother and sister at his lodgings, she 'sat down, almost shivering with terror, and gave the two ladies a timid look.' (Part III, Chapter 4).

Victim as martyr

At the same time Dostoyevsky emphasizes the self-sacrificing aspect of Sonya's character which accepts such victimization, even from her own step-mother:

> Beat me! Oh merciful Lord! And what if she did beat me – what then? What does it matter? You don't know anything, anything … She's so unhappy, oh, so unhappy!
>
> (Part IV, Chapter 4)

The whole issue hinges on the awareness of the role of women in the implementation of their own downfall. Sonya as a victim is at the mercy of her own emotional identification with the plight of others. It induces her to take on the emotional weight of Raskolnikov's secret confession. In her tormented grief and horror she becomes a victim all over again, articulating the responses which Raskolnikov fails to generate on his own account. Dunya is likewise perceived as a self-imposed martyr, forced to agree to a marriage of convenience (with Pyotr Petrovich) to ameliorate her mother's financial difficulties.

Dostoyevsky does not remain content with a simple exposé of victimization. Svidrigailov's encounter with the lost little girl turns into a nightmarish revelation of perverted innocence:

> He suddenly fancied that the long, black lashes of one of her eyes were quivering and blinking, that they were being raised and that from under them a sly, sharp little eye was peeping out, winking in a most unchildlike fashion.
>
> (Part VI, Chapter 6)

The issue of women as victims and martyrs ultimately conditions both the development of the narrative and its outcome. As Straus confirms:

> 'Woman' is a dominant fetish of Raskolnikov's culture, constituted by her lack of phallic, social, and political power.'
>
> (Straus, N., *Dostoyevsky and the Woman Question*, 1994,
> St Martin's Press, New York)

It is partly his sense of guilt over Dunya's impending marriage that impels Raskolnikov to resort to murder. His decision to confess to the authorities is prompted by his agonized response to her potential victimization. Svidrigailov has threatened to use his knowledge of Raskolnikov's crime as a form of blackmail to force Dunya to yield to him.

Redemption as an antidote

Dostoyevsky ends up by making use of the formulaic romantic device of the faithful woman who wins her man. It does establish some sense of ultimate justification for Sonya's long-term endurance. Her patient, long unappreciated devotion to Raskolnikov's welfare during his imprisonment finally induces him to reconsider his own priorities in life. But the overall theme of woman as victim continues as a recurrent strand in *The Idiot* and *The Brothers Karamazov*, suggesting that his solution for this salient issue was by no means a satisfactory one.

The resentful victim

Nastasya is the victimized woman in *The Idiot*, but she doesn't seem to conform to the usual prototypes. Her story is a typical chronicle of male lust and hypocrisy, not unlike the interpolated story of Marie which Myshkin relates to the Yepanchin women (Part I, Chapter 2). The most obvious non-conformity of Nastasya lies in her response to the treatment she endures. Forced into the position of a concubine through her ignorance and utter dependence on her guardian, she is portrayed as a woman torn by conflicting feelings of resentment and guilt. Sonya and Marie were passive, suffering victims; Nastasya protests and condemns, seeking revenge by broadcasting her humiliation. By way of making some excuse for refusing Myshkin's offer of marriage, she confesses:

> And then this man would come, stay two months in the year, bringing shame, dishonour, corruption, degradation, and go away.
>
> (Part I, Chapter 16)

Her need to publish her shame is equally nourished by an undiminished sense of her guilt and lack of self-esteem. The decision to run off with Rogozhin after the climactic scene at her name-day party is prompted by both factors. In fact, Ptitsyn finds a gruesome but extremely apt analogy for her conduct when he describes how the Japanese respond to insults by disembowelling themselves in the presence of their enemies (Part I, Chapter 16).

The 'femme fatale'

As a 'fallen woman', the victim shunned by society, Nastasya would hardly possess the same charismatic presence without her alluring beauty. She epitomizes 'the woman to die for', the temptress, the 'femme fatale' of romanticism. In such terms, Nastasya is also the woman who can exploit her attractions to obtain power in retaliation for her treatment. Her victims include Ganya, General Yepanchin and Rogozhin, all of whom seem to be capable of doing anything to obtain her favour. The coexistence of victim and predator in one woman creates a curious sense of incongruity, leading Aglaya to accuse her of 'posing as a fallen angel' out of vanity (Part III, Chapter 8). It becomes quite hard for the reader to decide whether to sympathize with her plight or condemn what could be described as a self-indulgent immersion in her grievances. Grushenka, in *The Brothers Karamazov*, is another extreme example of the ambivalent 'femme fatale', equally intent upon demonstrating her power. After a gushing emotional scene of reconciliation with Katya, she astonishes her rival by exclaiming:

Grushenka humiliates Katya.

> Now, you see, worthy young lady, how wicked and wilful I am next to you. Whatever I want, I will do.
>
> (Part I, Book III, Chapter 10)

Striving to find a voice

The capricious behaviour of Grushenka is typical of Dostoyevsky's female characters. The writer is so aware of the conflicting influences of different situations and contexts on personality and behaviour. What this does for the more complex women in his novels is to foreground the problems which they confront. Dostoyevsky portrays women who are striving to find a voice in a world which is essentially dominated by men. They can articulate their needs, to an extent, but lack the power to take positive action. In their struggles, they vacillate, contradict themselves, resort to duplicity. Or, like Sonya, they abjure, endure and pray. Aglaya reacts to an over-protective family by falling for Myshkin and finally marrying a scoundrel. Nastasya flees from one lover to another and Grushenka clings to the man who expresses the most determination to keep her.

A woman with potential

In *The Brothers Karamazov*, Katya is the first 'heroine' who begins to demonstrate a more assertive and influential position in relation to her world. Katya has the courage to acknowledge her catastrophic emotional lapse in the courtroom, an incident which virtually ensures Mitya's conviction. She risks public censure by taking charge of Ivan's welfare and develops plans for Mitya's escape. Her final reunion with Mitya demonstrates her ability to reconcile past experiences with her present situation:

> You now love another, I love another, but still I shall love you eternally, and you me, did you know that?
>
> (Epilogue, Chapter 2)

Such an assertion belongs to a woman who is beginning to assume her legitimate place in society. In *A Writer's Diary*, a few years before publishing *The Brothers Karamazov*, Dostoyevsky makes an urgent appeal to his fellow countrymen:

> Can we really continue to deny her, that woman who has so graphically displayed her valour, full equality of rights with men in education, employment, and official positions, when it is upon her that all our hopes now rest.
>
> (September, 1877, *A Writer's Diary*, Vol. II, Quartet Books (1995))

In this context the vociferous women who make such an impact on Dostoyevsky's novels; the victims, martyrs and fallen women, articulate a protest against the position of women in the society of his time. They are women poised on the brink of the first steps towards emancipation.

✴ ✴ ✴ ✴SUMMARY ✴ ✴ ✴ ✴

- Dostoyevsky's characters all show:

  - a great restlessness partly induced by constraints in their lives

  - a provisional attitude to their lives through their alienation and incessant movement

  - the best and worst qualities of human nature.

- Perfect goodness in a character represents an ultimate condition in a scale ranging from dark to light.

- Dostoyevsky's unresolved thoughts are never completely resolved: his perfection lies in the comprehensive nature of his enquiry.

- Woman as victim is a dominant theme in *Crime and Punishment*.

- *The Brothers Karamazov* develops the theme of the 'femme fatale' and victimized woman.

- Women in Dostoyevsky's novels express a development from victimization to the beginnings of autonomy.

- Settings are significant in what they tell us about Dostoyevsky's characters.

Contemporary critical responses

A FALSE START

The story of Dostoyevsky's sudden projection into the limelight reads like a writer's dream come true. 'A new Gogol has appeared!' exclaimed the poet Nekrasov as he burst into the office of the renowned critic Belinsky (Dostoyevsky, F., 1877, trans. Lantz, K., *A Writer's Diary*, Vol. II, p. 842).

He had just been spending the whole night reading through the manuscript of *Poor Folk* with a friend and had gone to congratulate Dostoyevsky at four o'clock that morning. 'You find Gogols springing up like mushrooms', remarked the more skeptical Belinsky. It didn't take long, however, for him to realize that, this time, Nekrasov was right.

> Only a genius with the insight to grasp in one minute what it takes an ordinary man many years to understand could write such a book at the age of twenty-five.
>
> (Grossmann, L., 1974, trans. Mackler, M., *Dostoyevsky*,
> Allen Lane, p.63)

The seal of approval from this influential critic was a guaranteed step on the ladder to fame. Dostoyevsky was swept into the circle of Belinsky's literary aficionados, feted and eulogized to his heart's content and more. He was introduced to the celebrated writer Turgenev and many aristocratic literary patrons.

Nekrasov published the novel in his journal, Belinsky offered him tips on how to succeed as a writer. 'Cherish your gift, remain true to it, and you will be a greater writer', he pronounced (*ibid*, p. 66). This was quite enough to turn the head of an inexperienced young writer, especially when his overwhelming success with the public seemed to confirm the sentiments of the critics.

DISILLUSIONMENT

When Dostoyevsky published 'The Landlady' not long afterwards, Belinsky seemed to have changed his mind about the young writer's ability. He thought the work was too derivative. Another long story, 'Mr Prokharchin' possessed only 'sparks of talent'. 'The Double'

Dostoyevsky – The person who apes his upper class betters.

received similar criticism, prompting Turgenev to write a satirical spoof, a caricature of Dostoyevsky. The rift between Dostoyevsky and Belinsky's clique was clearly more than a difference of opinion over some stories. In any case, Belinsky had moved away from the more idealistic stance that had attracted Dostoyevsky to his circle in the first place. Belinsky now favoured a more prosaic brand of realism in writing, an attitude which antagonized Dostoyevsky. Influenced by the writings of **Fourier** in his controversial *The New World of Industry and Society*, Dostoyevsky had become more sympathetic towards the ideals of **utopian socialism**. He reproached Belinsky for reducing literature solely to a description of newspaper reports and scandalous happenings. Overall, Dostoyevsky became utterly disillusioned with his former champions. Quarrelling with the renowned critic, he also managed to arouse the hostility of most of Belinsky's circle.

KEYWORDS

Utopian socialism: a socialist movement designed to reform society according to an ideal model. The most popular form of utopian socialism in Russia during the mid-nineteenth century was based on the socialist writings of Charles Fourier.

Confirmation of Belinsky's retraction in a letter to a fellow critic in 1848 was the last straw: 'We made a big mistake with Dostoyevsky when we called him "a genius"' (Sekirin, P.,1997, *The Dostoyevsky Archive*, McFarland & Company).

HIS REVENGE

Dostoyevsky become more reconciled to Belinsky just before the critic died in 1849, but he never quite relinquished his attitude towards Turgenev. Years later he featured a satirical portrait of Turgenev as the writer Karmazinov in his novel *The Possessed*. By then Dostoyevsky was able to muster additional grounds for complaint. He regarded Turgenev as a 'zapadnik', or Westernizer, meaning a Russian who preferred European culture to his own. The sense of a class distinction between his own penniless state and that of the 'gentry' writers such as Turgenev and Tolstoy was another issue he was very sensitive about. Dostoyevsky was well aware that he was always paid less for his work than either of his aristocratic colleagues. Even at the height of his considerable prestige as a writer, he earned only 300 rubles per quire for *The Brothers Karamazov*, considerably less than Turgenev could command.

ALTERNATIVE SUPPORTERS

It would be mistaken to assume that the capricious Belinsky ruined Dostoyevsky's early reputation. The injured writer soon became part of a circle of writers and scientists led by Valerian Maikov, a painter and influential literary critic. He admired Dostoyevsky's work and was in the process of writing a monograph on him which was only interrupted by his sudden death. Maikov was probably the first person to contradict a prevailing notion that Dostoyevsky was another Gogol in the making. He maintained that while Gogol was a social poet, Dostoyevsky's work was mainly psychological in content.

A NEW LEASE OF LIFE

After his enforced exile and imprisonment, Dostoyevsky was able to obtain permission to publish the journal *Vremya* (*The Times*), an enterprise he shared with his brother. What was significant about his function as an editor is the way it developed his own ability to respond to the ethos of the period. Writing and publishing writing became part of a rhythm, a continuous interchange of external stimuli, response and feedback. Some major influences stem from this time. For example, *Vremya* became a vehicle for the literary group known as the *pochva* (literally, soil), a 'back-to-basics' movement which emerged after the official emancipation of the serfs in 1861. *Pochva* trod a moderate path, advocating a bourgeois supported monarchy, aiming to promote a reconciliation of urban society with its peasant roots.

Another major influence came through Apollon Grigoryev, a charismatic critic and leading contributor to *Vremya*, who promoted drama as the ideal vehicle of communication with ordinary people. Significantly, this is the period when Dostoyevsky began to give public readings of his novels. They were received with enthusiasm, especially by younger audiences. Of course, the opportunities to publish his own works in *Vremya* were not neglected. *Memoirs from the House of the Dead* and *The Insulted and the Injured* were both circulated during the life of this journal.

A CONTROVERSIAL SUCCESS

Crime and Punishment (1866) was the novel that endorsed Dostoyevsky's reputation as a writer, yet once again there were setbacks. Published in a journal called *The Russian Messenger*, the first part achieved an instant success, becoming the literary sensation of the year. Subsequent instalments met with more criticism. For a start, the publisher objected to Sonya becoming a prostitute in order to keep her family from starving. Also, there were many critics who misinterpreted the characterization of Raskolnikov. Strakov, a supportive friend and critic, was the only person who seemed to understand what Dostoyevsky had in mind. He observed that Dostoyevsky:

> Shows us for the first time a nihilist who is unhappy, a nihilist who suffers deeply and humanly … The author has taken nihilism and carried it to its extreme … His aim was to show how life and theory struggle within a human soul, to depict that conflict in a situation in which it has reached its highest pitch, and to demonstrate that in the end life wins out.

> (Grossmann, L., 1974, *Dostoyevsky*, Allen Lane, p.355)

CONFIRMATION OF SUCCESS

Dostoyevsky's novels continued to attract considerable attention, even during his years abroad, and he was beginning to be recognized as one of Russia's leading writers of the period. *The Idiot*, published in book form at the end of 1873, was sold out in just two days. Another indication of his popularity is the success of the journal *A Writer's Diary*, published between 1872 and 1881. Dostoyevsky first began to incorporate this type of feuilleton style journal into *The Citizen*. It proved to be so successful that he was soon able to launch the journal as an independent enterprise. *A Writer's Diary* became a household name throughout Russia, generating a stream of correspondence from its readers. In 1877 Dostoyevsky was finally able to gain permission from the Ministry of the Press to publish the work without the usual constraints of censorship. This had been a major obstacle to the success of his previous journals.

THE PUSHKIN OVATION

By 1880 Dostoyevsky's popularity surpassed that of any of his literary rivals. He had just released his concluding episode of *The Brothers Karamazov* to considerable popular acclaim. This was also the year of his Pushkin commemoration speech, an occasion that confirmed what had become the virtual cult status of Dostoyevsky in the eyes of the public. Pushkin and Dostoyevsky were both writers who seemed to be able to address people's hearts and to articulate a belief in Russian identity, qualities which were much needed at this time.

POSTHUMOUS REPUTATION

After the lengthy funeral commemorations for Dostoyevsky had ended, the voices of dissenting critics made themselves heard once again. Dostoyevsky was almost as controversial figure in death as he had been in life. In *A Cruel Talent*, a monograph published just a year after Dostoyevsky's death, the activist and literary critic Mikhailovsky attacked him for his reactionary views and his passion for suffering. Tolstoy himself voiced his concern over the issue of:

> Raising to the level of prophet and saint a man who died in the midst of a most heated inner struggle between good and evil. He is moving, interesting, but you cannot take a man who was all struggle, and set him up on a monument for the instruction of posterity.
>
> (Grossmann, L.,1974, *Dostoyevsky, A Biography*, Allen Lane, p.552)

In any case, the posthumous reputation of Dostoyevsky was never a matter of unanimous agreement. Most of his favourable critics had their own agenda and concentrated on aspects of his work which suited their concerns. Soloviev (1853–1900), a close friend and critical philosopher, believed that all his writing represented a striving towards a kind of true socialism. He maintained that Dostoyevsky expressed a sense of Russian identity through a regeneration of society and a renewal of spiritual values. Rozanov (1863–1919), another philosopher and literary critic, wrote a major work on 'The Legend of the Grand Inquisitor' (*The Brothers Karamazov*). He admired Dostoyevsky so much that he ended up marrying his former mistress, Apollinaria Suslova. Volynsky (1863–1926), a symbolist literary critic, explored Dostoyevsky's concepts of beauty, pointing out the way Dostoyevsky challenged conventional notions of beauty as a characteristic of goodness. The variety of interpretations which seemed to be justifiable for such a complex writer also made his works susceptible to criticism and censorship. After the Russian Revolution, the works of Dostoyevsky were blacklisted on political grounds and re-introduced in Russia only during the 1950s.

✷ ✷ ✷ ✷SUMMARY ✷ ✷ ✷ ✷

- Dostoyevsky's early 'discovery' gave him a false illusion of success.

- His subsequent rejection by Belinsky and his clique was a source of bitterness to him.

- Dostoyevsky found acceptance with Maikov and his circle.

- After his years of exile, he became a successful editor and was published again to considerable acclaim.

- The Pushkin Ovation marked the height of his popularity.

- The complexity of his work made it susceptible to censorship.

Modern critical approaches: voices and vision

PSYCHOANALYTIC CRITICISM

Sigmund Freud changed the way we look at ourselves through his innovative development of an approach to psychology which he called psychoanalysis. He also had a tremendous influence on the way we examine literature. What he did was to translate his methods of clinical psychoanalysis into a diagnostic approach towards the analysis of literary texts. Freud believed that all concealment is suppressed desire which is revealed through the characters and events in a narrative. He therefore concentrated on revealing the hidden content of any literary work. This became known as **psychoanalytic criticism**. Freud's clinical interest in Dostoyevsky found direct expression in his essay on parricide (Freud, S., 1961, 'Dostoyevsky and Parricide', *Standard Edition of the Collected Psychological Works*, Hogarth Press, Vol. XXI, pp.177–94). In this concentrated essay he examines the significance of parricide in Dostoyevsky's

> **KEYWORD**
>
> Psychoanalytic criticism: using the processes of psychoanalysis developed by Freud as a method of analysis for literary texts.

personal life and its application to *The Brothers Karamazov*. As an introduction to Freud's methods of psychoanalytic criticism, it could be the ideal place to start.

Parricide as a theme

> It can scarcely be owing to chance that three of the masterpieces of the literature of all time – the *Oedipus Rex* of Sophocles, Shakespeare's *Hamlet* and Dostoevsky's *The Brothers Karamazov* – should all deal with the same subject: parricide.
>
> (Freud, S., 1961, 'Dostoyevsky and Parricide', *Standard Edition of the Collected Psychological Works*, Hogarth Press, Vol. XXI, pp.177.)

A contentious statement, pronounced with the confidence of an authority. It not only clarifies the status that Freud attributes to Dostoyevsky's work, but confirms his view of the significance of a psychoanalytic approach to the study of literature.

Freud's essay outlines his proposition that parricide in Dostoyevsky is a confessional theme expressing problems which he experienced in his childhood. His argument is developed through his analysis of the relationship between parricide and Dostoyevsky's epileptic condition.

Epilepsy as a symptom of neurosis

Freud regards Dostoyevsky's epilepsy as a symptom of a neurosis rather than a physiological condition. Such a presumption leads him to the conclusion that his so-called epileptic seizures were actually a manifestation of severe hysteria, which he describes as a discharge of stimuli accumulated in a state of intense excitement. The energy expended is not unlike the experience of having sex. He traces Dostoyevsky's epilepsy back to his childhood traumas, a time when he was subject to periods of intense melancholy and an irrational fear of death.

Castration complex

Freud interprets this phobia about death as an identification with someone who is dead or whom the subject wishes dead. Through a process of psychological **transference**, the desire for someone else's death can become a punishment inflicted on oneself. Freud uses references to Dostoyevsky's strained relationship with his father to argue that Dostoyevsky hated him and desired his death. Fear of his father, apparently a violent man, resulted in a **repression** of the desire for his death. What was **projected** instead was his intense melancholy and fear of his own death.

KEYWORDS

Transference: the process by which feelings originally directed at significant figures from childhood are later in life directed towards others. These 'others' are treated *as if they were* the earlier significant figures.

Repression: the active exclusion of an unwelcome thought from unconscious awareness.

In Freudian terms, this is a classic case of a **castration complex**. Freud cites the violent death of Dostoyevsky's father as the catalyst that induced his first epileptic fits, a condition which he perceives as a pathological development of this childhood sublimation.

The Oedipus complex in Dostoyevsky

The epilepsy in Dostoyevsky is reinforced by what Freud considers his bisexual disposition, a repressed feminine attitude exemplified by Freud in his theories of the **Oedipus complex**. This he explains not in terms of Dostoyevsky's relationship to his mother, but more significantly in terms of his desire to enter into the kind of relationship which his mother experienced with his father. This is basically passive and **masochistic**, a suitable medium for the self-inflicted punishment which his castration complex requires. Freud draws attention to the significance of male friendships to Dostoyevsky and his sympathy

KEYWORDS

Projection: the unconscious transfer of one's own impressions or feelings to external objects or persons.

Castration complex: a term used by Freud to identify a condition induced by a son's fear of his father's potentially harmful anger.

Oedipus complex: the desire of the son directed towards his mother, emerging in a longing to replace the father or in a desire to obtain the mother's emotional subjugation to the father.

Masochism: a form of perversion based on the gratification of one's own pain or humiliation.

with his rivals in love as an indication of latent homosexuality. He notices that some of Dostoyevsky's characters express ambivalence about their own sexuality. No doubt he has Myshkin in mind who, in *The Idiot*, tells Ganya that he cannot marry due to his condition (Part I, Chapter 3).

The Brothers Karamazov as confession

In these terms Freud is able to interpret *The Brothers Karamazov* as a form of authorial confession of his desire to commit parricide. The murder of Fyodor Pavlovich is actually committed by the half-brother of Dmitri, whose professed intention to murder his father was common knowledge. It is a form of murder by proxy which is kept within the family, just as if Dmitri had done it himself as far as Freud is concerned. Sexual jealousy and rivalry for the same woman are dominant motifs open to Freudian interpretation. Moreover, as Freud points out in relation to Smerdyakov:

> It is a remarkable fact that Dostoyevsky has attributed to him his own illness, the alleged epilepsy, as though he were seeking to confess that the epileptic, the neurotic, in himself was a parricide.
>
> (Freud, S., 1962, *Dostoyevsky*, Prentice-Hall, p.107–8)

Whether or not one can accept this idea, it is significant that the conclusions reached by Freud seem to reinforce the ethical issues of guilt and responsibility which Dostoyevsky himself explores throughout the narrative:

> It is a matter of indifference who actually committed the crime; psychology is only concerned to know who desired it emotionally and who welcomed it when it was done. And for that reason all of the brothers, except the contrasted figure of Alyosha, are equally guilty.
>
> (*ibid*, p.108)

'Dostoyevsky and Parricide' represents an innovative attempt to interpret the work of Dostoyevsky with a new 'set of tools'. Has Freud any further contributions to make which are relevant to the study of Dostoyevsky's works?

The double

The theme of the double fascinated Dostoyevsky. He published an early work, a novella called *The Double* (1846), which was poorly received, but the idea remained one of abiding interest to him. Freud was the first to formulate in psychoanalytic terms the concept of the double as a projection of an unpleasant part of the hidden self (1919, 'Essay on the Uncanny', *Complete Psychological Works of Sigmund Freud*, Vol. XVII, Hogarth Press). Sometimes this projection becomes an alien double identity, assuming a demoniacal form. The application of this idea to Ivan's conversation with the devil in *The Brothers Karamazov* can hardly be ignored (Part IV, Bk 11, Chapter 9). In fact, Dostoyevsky seems to have anticipated Freud, for Ivan is well aware of his own relationship to this phantom devil.

The uncanny

In the same essay, Freud's concept of the uncanny offers a rationale for some of Dostoyevsky's extraordinary scenes in which reality and fantasy seem to merge. In many of these scenes it is hard to establish where ordinary life is replaced by something imagined. Freud describes the uncanny as 'that class of the frightening which leads back to what is known of old and long familiar' (1919, 'Essay on the Uncanny', *Complete Psychological Works of Sigmund Freud*, Vol. XVII, Hogarth Press, p.220). Such an explanation could offer a rationale for the interpretation of Svidrigailov's wanderings in *Crime and Punishment* (Part VI, Chapter 6) or Ippolyt's reported experience of Rogozhin's nocturnal visit in *The Idiot* (Part III, Chapter 5). There is a particular discomfort in the discovery that the familiar is actually not so familiar and Dostoyevsky was particularly skilled in his use of this phenomenon.

Disadvantages of Freudian analysis

Freud's perception of the significance of parricide in the context of Dostoyevsky's life and work remains a controversial if somewhat reductive account of the relationship between neurosis and creative development. The problem with such an approach is that facts can so easily lend themselves to the support of theories based on hypothetical truths. Catteau asserts that 'Freudian analysis, based on obscure and unprovable data, has arbitrarily distorted his life and character' (1989, *Dostoyevsky and the Process of Literary Creation*, Cambridge University Press, p.2). Breger confirms that Dostoyevsky was suffering from temporal-lobe epilepsy and refutes Freud's clinical diagnosis:

> 'Hysterical epilepsy' is a recognizable entity today; it appears in patients who mimic, or act out, seizures, almost always before an audience. It is clear that Dostoevsky did not have this particular condition; his seizures

mainly occurred during sleep when he was alone. What is more, he suffered physical injury from them, something that does not occur in hysterical epilepsy.

(Breger, L., 1989, *Dostoevsky: The Author as Psychoanalyst*,
New York University Press, p.241)

Does this diagnosis invalidate Freud's psychoanalytic approach to Dostoyevsky?

Psychoanalytic theory and Dostoyevsky

Given the enormous influence of Freud in the field of literary criticism, it seems appropriate to take his methods into account, but to accept his own conclusions about Dostoyevsky with some reservations. Contemporary psychoanalytic criticism concentrates on the influential concepts developed by Freud but finds less diagnostic ways to apply them. In the analysis of Dostoyevsky's work, Elizabeth Dalton, for example, makes use of Freud's concept of the **superego** for her discussion of Myshkin's epilepsy (Dalton, E., 1979, 'The Epileptic Mode of Being', *Unconscious Structure in 'The Idiot'. A Study in Literature and Psychoanalysis*, Princeton University Press). Louis Breger believes that it is more constructive to shed the Freudian concept of the author as a patient and

KEYWORD

Superego: that part of the mind which acts as a conscience and responds to social rules.

reconsider the author in terms of a fellow psychoanalyst. The fundamental relationship between the psychosis of the author and the analysis of the text is still an important factor. However, the text is equally open to interpretation in terms of more than one psychological perspective. This makes a lot of sense in the light of Dostoyevsky's multiple points of view and his ability to write through the perspective of a range of characters.

Relevance of Freud

Freud's own interpretation of Dostoyevsky may be criticized, but his innovative concepts remain valuable tools for a penetrating analysis of character, author and text. As an approach to literature, psychoanalytic criticism bridges the gap between psychology and literature, opening up the field of potential interpretation to include the complex study of neuroses, the relationship of the reader to the text and the analysis of the language of the text itself. In the broader context of literary criticism, the contributions of Freud have activated approaches to criticism which continue to make a viable contribution towards our understanding of Dostoyevsky's work.

BAKHTIN AND DIALOGIC CRITICISM

Much critical attention to Dostoyevsky's writing is based around the work of Mikhail Bakhtin. It was only in the 1980s, after years of exile, that translations of his works became widely available in the West. Since then, Bakhtin has been acclaimed as a precursor of modern literary criticism, his methods adopted in an approach which has become known as **dialogic criticism**.

> **KEYWORD**
>
> Dialogic criticism: an approach to literary criticism modelled on the ideas of Bakhtin. He argued that a text is characterized by the interaction and inter-dependence of different elements or multiple voices.

His unique artistic vision

Bakhtin was not just another literary theorist. What is exciting about his ideas is their more fundamental insight into a mode of being. In *Problems of Dostoyevsky's Poetics*, Bakhtin moves beyond a critical theoretical domain to emphasize the unique creative vision of Dostoyevsky.

Bakhtin affirms that Dostoyevsky offered a distinctive and totally original perception of the world, based on an awareness of the relativity of a given situation. He argues that most writers have sought to establish a monological or one-sided viewpoint towards their subject. An analogy would be that of an artist who composes and executes a painting in which all the elements are resolved according to a pre-conceived scheme. The author formulates and executes a novel like this artist, creating a cohesive plot, distinct and clearly defined characters and a resolved ending. The opposite approach is adopted by the artists who create their works in a more open-ended way, allowing chance elements to intervene and influence the development of the composition, superimposing more than one perception of the subject. Bakhtin believes that Dostoyevsky was innovative in his introduction of a multi-dimensional perspective into his novels. Instead of entering the narrative space of the author, the reader is often able to perceive events according to the shifting perspectives of the characters themselves. Bakhtin employs a musical term to describe these multiple levels of interaction.

Many voices of the polyphonic novel

The term **polyphonic** is applied to a musical form in which two or more independent voices have equal significance. In adopting the term '**polyphonic novel**' to describe those of Dostoyevsky, Bakhtin was not making an arbitrary connection, for he knew that Dostoyevsky had considered a relationship between his work and musical counterpoint (another form of polyphony). In any case, the concept of polyphony seems to explain so clearly the methods of Dostoyevsky's approach:

KEYWORDS

Polyphonic: pertaining to music characterized by the interweaving of many voices, sometimes referred to as counterpoint.

Polyphonic novel: a novel in which characters and events can be described in terms of their co-existence and interaction.

> A plurality of independent and unmerged voices and consciousnesses, a genuine polyphony of fully valid voices is in fact the chief characteristic of Dostoyevsky's novels.
>
> (Bakhtin, M., 1984, *Problems of Dostoyevsky's Poetics*,
> Manchester University Press, p.6)

Characters in themselves have many voices or many facets of personality and behaviour. They can be contradictory, elusive, moody and unpredictable. Furthermore, they come together in situations which generate extraordinary interactions and conflicts, creating cascading scenes and events which add to the polyphonic dimensions of the narrative. Instead of trying to organize, prioritize or eliminate these accumulating incidents, Dostoyevsky seems to allow them to compete for the attention of the reader almost indiscriminately, until they converge in his notorious scandal scenes. Such an intensive condensation of events adds further complexity to the narrative pace, distorting the sense of real time.

The carnival

Bakhtin sees Dostoyevsky's writing as the means by which he represents and examines the world of his experience. This can take the form of a challenging interrogation, even a form of debunking of stereotypical attitudes and modes of behaviour. In *Problems of Dostoyevsky's Poetics*, he formulates a concept of the **carnivalesque** and identifies a traditional genre, both of which help to explain the extraordinary process by which this is achieved.

Menippean satire featured extended dialogues and debates, often set in the context of banquets or parties. The assembled company of assorted individuals reinforced the absurdity of their attitudes by the arguments they used. A resemblance to scenes in Dostoyevsky's novels can hardly be ignored! In a more generic sense, the carnivalesque invokes a sense of relativity and absurdity through the use of extreme contrasts. This is the upside-down world of inside-out perception, celebrating the diversity of an extraordinary world. Bakhtin identifies a carnivalesque approach in the works of Rabelais, Sterne and Voltaire during the eighteenth century. He also cites Hoffmann and Edgar Allen Poe, Balzac, Sand, Hugo and

KEYWORDS

Carnivalesque: a term derived from ancient festivals of the classical world, used by Bakhtin to describe a literary tradition based on satire, parody and the absurd.

Menippean satire: a form of indirect satire derived from a Greek form developed by the Cynic philosopher Menippus. Examples of Menippean satire in European literature include *Gargantua and Pantagruel* (1564) by Rabelais and Voltaire's *Candide* (1759).

Gogol, all nineteenth-century writers who inherited aspects of the carnivalesque. All of these writers had some influence on Dostoyevsky.

The carnivalesque in scandal scenes

Carnival is particularly evident in the scandal scenes which form such an intrinsic feature in the development of Dostoyevsky's narratives. Bakhtin notes that scandal scenes were frequently criticized during Dostoyevsky's lifetime and that they continue to attract controversy. However, he affirms that such scenes are not arbitrary or disorganized, but deeply organic in exposing the logic of carnival. Through the conflicts and interactions of these scenes, Dostoyevsky brings out the relativity of the events taking place. In scandal scenes nothing is absolute or determined. Characters and events are deliberately polarized, set in contrast to each other. A striking example of this occurs in *The Brothers Karamazov*. Dmitri and his father, during a visit to the monastery, are drawn into a violent quarrel in which even the monks are reviled and goaded into participation (Book II, Chapter 6). The conflict is interrupted at a critical moment when Father Zosima inexplicably kneels before Dmitri and bows to him.

Bakhtin's contribution to our understanding of Dostoyevsky

The dialogic theories of Bakhtin offer a coherent creative guide to the interpretation of some of the more difficult aspects of Dostoyevsky's writing. By isolating the concepts of polyphony and the carnivalesque, Bakhtin exposes the fundamental differences of approach to writing that is intrinsically creative. It is left up to the reader to take the opportunity to respond to Dostoyevsky's creative approach by adopting a more flexible and imaginative attitude towards interpretation.

Dialogic criticism and Dostoyevsky

Dialogic criticism takes this more flexible approach to interpretation quite seriously. The interaction of multiple voices and meanings in the literary text applies also to the coexistence of critical theories and approaches towards the text. This is not an excuse for the notion that 'anything goes', but an acknowledgment that the diverse approaches of literary criticism sustain an active debate which should never relapse into authoritarianism. (For a more recent critical response to Dostoyevsky based on the ideas of Bakhtin, refer to *Dostoyevsky after Bakhtin* by Malcolm Jones (Cambridge University Press, 1990).)

FEMINIST CRITICISM AND DOSTOYEVSKY

Straus has drawn attention to the rediscovery of Bakhtin in the West as an impetus in the development of feminist literary criticism. In *Dostoyevsky and the Woman Question* (1994, St Martin's Press) she uses a dialogic approach in her construction of a feminist critique of the novels of Dostoyevky. His concept of 'the feminine' is perceived by Straus as a problem which mirrors his own confusion about the meaning of masculinity. Straus also discusses the significance of her observation that women in Dostoyevsky:

> Carry what is least representable, least vocalized, most marginal, but also most modernist in his fiction.
>
> (1994, *Dostoevsky and the Woman Question*, St Martin's Press, p.2)

A RANGE OF RESPONSES

Psychoanalytic, dialogic and feminist criticism are just some of the critical approaches which can be used to illuminate aspects of Dostoyevsky's works. Given the versatility, the multiple perspectives and imaginative range of his work, it is hardly surprising to discover a corresponding range of critical responses in our time. André Gide wrote a penetrating monograph on Dostoyevsky (1967, Penguin Books) celebrating his capacity for creating art out of the complexity and confusion of life. He admired Dostoyevsky for his refusal to construct a sense of harmony by a false imposition of order. For an accessible critical account of the unique contribution of Dostoyevsky to the development of the novel, it can hardly be surpassed. In *Tolstoy or Dostoyevsky: An Essay in the Old Criticism* (1996, Yale University Press), George Steiner discusses the thematic issues raised by a comparison of these two contrasting writers. Additional critical responses to the works of Dostoyevsky can be found in edited editions such as *New Essays on Dostoyevsky* (Jones, M. and Terry, G., eds, 1990, Cambridge University Press). *Reading Dostoevsky* (Terras, V., 1999, University of Wisconsin Press) is the most recent accessible study of his life and works.

Readers who find the enormous range of critical works on Dostoyevsky somewhat daunting would do well to concentrate on some of the introductory sections to the publications of his major novels. Keith Carabine's introduction to *Crime and Punishment* (2000, Wordsworth Classics) is a helpful one which even contains a map of St Petersburg locating the sites described in the novel. Alternatively, *The Dostoyevsky Archive*, (1997, McFarland & Company) captures a sense of intimacy and a genuine flavour of the period. It is full of reminiscences by people who actually knew Dostoyevsky.

＊＊＊＊SUMMARY ＊＊＊＊

- Parricide is a theme which Freud links to Dostoyevsky's condition of epilepsy.

- Freud diagnoses the epilepsy of Dostoyevsky as a symptom of neurosis originating in childhood trauma.

- Freud believes that a castration complex was the fundamental cause of Dostoyevsky's epilepsy.

- Psychoanalytic criticism today develops the application of Freud's theories through a less diagnostic exploration of author, character and text.

- Bakhtin argues that Dostoyevsky created a new model of artistic vision.

- In the polyphonic novels of Dostoyevsky, multiple voices emerge through his concern to show the operation of conflicting forces in characters and events.

- Bakhtin develops a theory of the carnivalesque in which he drew on the tradition of Menippean satire as an indirect literary influence on Dostoyevsky.

Where next?

MANY POSSIBILITIES

Dostoyevsky was so creative and wide ranging in his approach that it is possible to pursue quite independent lines of enquiry in the selection of further reading. Since there are so many parallels between his writing and his life, however, it might be an idea to start with several works which are specifically drawn from events in his own past.

Life inside

Memoirs from the House of the Dead (1983, *World's Classics*, Oxford University Press) is presented as a novel but is basically an evocation of Dostoyevsky's own experiences of imprisonment. Taking into account the amendments he made to pass the censors, the work still remains a revealing disclosure of prison conditions at that time.

THE GAMBLER

The Gambler (1997, Norton) another novel that contains true-to-life autobiographical features was likewise transformed into an opera, this one by Sergei Prokofiev. The story of the circumstances under which Dostoyevsky wrote the novel, in itself, forms an account of melodramatic dimensions, as is the romance of the casinos on which it is based (see biography, p.14). In *Memoirs from the House of the Dead*, the prison walls imposed an obvious constraint upon the inmates. *The Gambler*, however, uses the lure of the game to exert its own compulsive conditions.

The short stories

Dostoyevsky's ability to draw on his life experience and imaginative powers alike adds a particularly fertile and inventive dynamic to his work. His early admiration for Edgar Allan Poe and E.T.A. Hoffmann is apparent in the stories which invoke the uncanny. 'Bobok', 'The

The dead talk to each other as in life.

Dream of a Ridiculous Man', 'A Fantastic Story', 'A Gentle Spirit' and 'White Nights' are additional stories which rely on a juxtaposition of paranormal or abnormal situations with ordinary life. For those with a taste for the absurd, however, 'The Crocodile' is perhaps the strangest story of all. Do not imagine that it has anything to do with a natural habitat!

CREATIVE RESPONSES

It is not always necessary to read literary criticism to learn about Dostoyevsky. A look at the creative stimulus of Dostoyevsky on the works of other writers is a fascinating alternative. J. M. Coetzee used biographical data and material from *The Possessed* to write his own novel *The Master of Petersburg* (1994). Albert Camus gave public confirmation of his admiration for Dostoyevsky in 1938 when he directed Copeau's adaptation of *The Brothers Karamazov*. Significantly, he himself played the part of Ivan, a character with whom he expressed his complete identification. In 1959 he wrote his own dramatized version of *The Possessed* (*Les Possédés*). His philosophical treatise, *The Myth of Sisyphus* (1942), has a substantial section devoted to a study of Dostoyevsky and *L'Homme Révolté* (1951) contains many further references.

DOSTOYEVSKY AND THE 'ABSURD'

Camus was particularly interested in translating Dostoyevsky's disjunctive perspective on life into his own philosophy of the 'absurd'. In Camus's terms, the absurd in life is borne out by the meaningless position of the individual in relation to conventional norms of society. Social interaction, customs, expressions of piety are perceived as hollow formalities devoid of real meaning. The recognition of the absurdity of life depends on an ability to find happiness without hope of immortality. Camus felt that Dostoyevsky had resorted to the Christian faith as a way of opting out of this necessity. He drew attention to the evidence of Dostoyevsky's letters, in which he admits that to his dying day he would be 'the child of disbelief and doubt' (Davison, R., 1997, *Camus: The Challenge of Dostoyevsky*, University of Exeter Press). In support of his ideas, Camus pointed out the significant role of Dostoyevsky's memorable 'rebel' characters such as Ivan (*The Brothers Karamazov*) and Stavrogin (*The Possessed*). Such characters, he felt, articulated the problem of coming to terms with their position in a world without God.

DOSTOYEVSKY AND THE CINEMA

The inspiration of Dostoyevsky is not confined to literature and philosophy. Filmmakers the world over have made use of Dostoyevsky's works as a fertile source of material. The universal dimension of his writing was recognized by the great Japanese director Akira Kurosawa. One of the earliest and most renowned adaptations of *The Idiot* is set in nineteenth-century Japan. Toshiro Mifune plays the former soldier and ex-patient with a history of mental illness and epilepsy. He travels from the tropical region of Okinawa to the wintery region of Hokaido 'seeking truth'. Falling in love with another man's mistress on the way, he finds himself living out an untruth, thus creating an insoluble dilemma for himself. In *The Return of the Idiot*, a contemporary film by Sasa Gedeon set in the Czech Republic, Frantisek is the epileptic innocent who demonstrates such uncomfortable insight into the problems of his friends.

Here is a list of selected films which gives some idea of their multinational range and diversity:

Batalov, Alexei, *The Gambler*, 1973 (Russia)
Brooks, Richard, *The Brothers Karamazov*, 1958 (USA)
Chenal, Pierre, *Crime and Punishment*, 1935 (first sound version) (France)
Kulidzhanov, Lev, *Crime and Punishment*, 1970 (Russia)
Kurosawa, Akira, *The Idiot* (*Hakuchi*) 1951 (Japan)
Gedeon, Sasa, *The Return of the Idiot*, 1999 (Czech)
Makk, Karoly, *The Gambler*, 1997 (GB)
Pyrev, Ivan, *The Brothers Karamazov*, 1968 *The Idiot*, 1957 (Russia)
Schmidt, Rob, *Crime and Punishment in Suburbia*, 2000 (USA)
Wajda, Andrzej, *Nastasja* 1994; *The Possessed*, 1988 (Poland)

DOSTOYEVSKY ON THE WEB

Browsing through the numerous websites devoted to Dostoyevsky can be a fascinating but not entirely rewarding task. There are a lot of enthusiasts out there with not much insight. The Dostoyevsky Research Station at www.kiosek.com/dostoevsky provides a good range of material in presentable format. For additional sources, try searching for Dostoyevsky using the various Internet search engines.

BACK TO DOSTOYEVSKY

Before all possibilities are exhausted it might prove more worthwhile to return to the works themselves. At the end of the day, the test of a great work is whether one can bear to read it again. Dostoyevsky's works seem not only to fulfil this brief but to yield more with subsequent readings. Like our closest friends, it sometimes takes a long time to get to know them. Dostoyevsky remains a writer who will always have something relevant to say to us about the human condition and our insufficient attempts to come to terms with the extraordinary world we inhabit.

✳ ✳ ✳ ✳SUMMARY ✳ ✳ ✳ ✳

- Dostoyevsky's short stories demonstrate his ability to integrate the real world with the imaginary.

- Dostoyevsky has stimulated a wide range of creative responses in our time.

- Camus is a notable example of a writer who was influenced by Dostoyevsky.

- Film-makers all over the world have been inspired by his works.

- His works have a relevance for us today.

Glossary

Carnivalesque   A term derived from ancient festivals of the classical world, used by Bakhtin to describe a literary tradition based on satire, parody and the absurd.

Castration complex   A term used by Freud to identify a condition induced by a son's fear of his father's potentially harmful anger.

Dialectic   Presenting opposite points of view in an argument in order to reach a conclusion.

Dialogic criticism   An approach to literary criticism modelled on the ideas of Bakhtin. He argued that a text is characterized by the interaction and interdependence of different elements or multiple voices.

Epistolary novel   A novel written in the style of letters exchanged between characters.

Feuilleton   A sequence of articles and anecdotes with an integrating commentary published in almanac form.

Feuilletons became popular during the 1840s in Europe.

Gothic fiction   A term used to describe fiction infused with a brooding atmosphere of gloom and terror reminiscent of the gothic novels of Anne Radcliffe, William Beckford and Matthew Lewis.

Holy Fool   This was the tradition of kenoticism which emerged in the Russian Orthodox Church during the fourteenth century, where the 'holy fool' practised a kind of radical asceticism, irrationality, could feign madness and was inspired by a gift of prophecy.

Interpolated narratives   Stories told by characters which interrupt, complement or digress from the main plot of the novel.

Masochism   A form of perversion based on the gratification of one's own pain or humiliation.

Menippean satire   A form of indirect satire derived from a Greek form developed by the Cynic philosopher Menippus. Examples of Menippean satire in

European literature include *Gargantua and Pantagruel* (1564) by Rabelais and Voltaire's *Candide* (1759).

Narodnik A person affiliated to a populist group that promoted education for the peasants and a back-to-basics approach to Russian culture.

Nietzsche A German philosopher (1844–1900) who argued that ideas and actions are given a reality through an assertion of 'will'. His works were published after 1872.

Nihilist A person who rejects all traditional religious and moral principles. Nihilists in Dostoyevsky's period also upheld extreme political views.

Oedipus complex The desire of the son directed towards his mother, emerging in a longing to replace the father or in a desire to obtain the mother's emotional subjugation to the father.

Polyphonic Pertaining to music characterized by the interweaving of many voices, sometimes referred to as counterpoint.

Polyphonic novel A novel in which characters and events can be described in terms of their coexistence and interaction.

Psychoanalytic criticism Using the processes of psychoanalysis developed by Freud as a method of analysis for literary texts.

Projection The unconscious transfer of one's own impressions or feelings to external objects or persons.

Proto-Nietzschean In anticipation of the ideas of Nietzsche.

Realistic novel Fictional attempt to convey the effect of realism through the interaction of characters of a specific social class in everyday situations.

Repression The active exclusion of an unwelcome thought from unconscious awareness.

Scandal scene A dramatic, disruptive encounter between two or more characters.

Superego That part of the mind which acts as a conscience and responds to social rules.

Totalitarianism   Relating to a centralized dictatorial form of government which demands complete subservience to the state.

Transference   The process by which feelings originally directed at significant figures from childhood are later in life directed towards others. These 'others' are treated *as if they were* the earlier significant figures.

Uncanny   The ordinary world made strange and sinister.

Utopian socialism   A socialist movement designed to reform society according to an ideal model. The most popular form of utopian socialism in Russia during the mid-nineteenth century was based on the socialist writings of **Charles Fourier.**

Chronology of major works

1845   *Poor Folk* completed. Acclaimed by Belinsky.

1846   *Poor Folk* and 'The Double' published. 'The Landlady' published.

1848   'White Nights' and other stories.

1860   Starts periodical *Vremya* (*The Times*) with his brother.

1861   Publishes *Memoirs from the House of the Dead*.

1864   Founds journal Epokha. It contains *Notes from Underground*.

1866   *Crime and Punishment*.

1867   *The Gambler*.

1868   *The Idiot*.

1870   *The Eternal Husband*.

1871   Publication of *The Possessed*, or *The Demons*.

1872   A Raw Youth.

1873   Editor of The Citizen. Beginning of *The Diary of a Writer* included.

1876   *The Diary of a Writer* – independent publication as a journal.

1879–80 *The Brothers Karamazov*.

Index